Deep Cut
by Philip Ralph

This play was commissioned by Sgript Cymru, produced by Sherman Cymru and first performed at Sherman, Cardiff, on Thursday 24 July, 2008.

TOUR

Sherman, Cardiff (Previews)   24 – 26 July

Traverse Theatre, Edinburgh   31 July – 24 August

Clwyd Theatr Cymru, Mold   9 - 13 September

Sherman, Cardiff   16 – 27 September

CAST

DES JAMES	Ciaran McIntyre
DOREEN JAMES	Rhian Morgan
BRIAN CATHCART / LIEUTENANT COLONEL NIGEL JOSLING	Robert Bowman
NICHOLAS BLAKE QC	Simon Molloy
FRANK SWANN / BRUCE GEORGE MP	Robert Blythe
JONESY	Rhian Blythe

PRODUCTION TEAM

WRITER	Philip Ralph
DIRECTOR	Mick Gordon
DESIGNER	Igor Vasiljev
LIGHTING DESIGNER	Andrew Jones
SOUND DESIGNER	Mike Furness
ASSISTANT DIRECTOR	Juliane Von Sivers
PRODUCTION MANAGER	Nick Allsop
COMPANY STAGE MANAGER	Brenda Knight
DEPUTY STAGE MANAGER	Natasha White
ASSISTANT STAGE MANAGER	Kirsty Louise Airlie
WARDROBE MANAGER	Deryn Tudor
SET CONSTRUCTION	Alan Turner & Matthew Thomas
SENIOR CARPENTER	Ian George
DESIGN ASSISTANT	Charlotte Neville
CASTING	Kate Perridge

THANKS

Rumney High School, Cardiff; RSM Carl Roberts of Maindy Barracks; Marilyn le Conte and the Royal Welsh College of Music and Drama; Des and Doreen James; Amy Ball; Josie Anthony Dray & Nick Dray.

SHERMAN
CYMRU

We aim to produce and present ambitious, compelling theatre and believe in the potency of theatre to inspire and transform.

We strive to create the best theatre we can; to achieve a distinct and diverse programme for our audiences; to engage our communities in the creative process of theatre making; and to make a lasting contribution to the national and international development of theatre in Wales and the vigour of theatre in its capital city.

We produce work in both English and Welsh, and tour widely within Wales and the UK. *Deep Cut* is our fourth premiere of new work since Sherman Cymru was created in April 2007 through the merger of Sgript Cymru and the Sherman Theatre Company.

> 'This unmissable drama...promises much for the future of
> new writing company Sherman Cymru'
> *The Guardian* on Kaite O'Reilly's *The Almond and The Seahorse*

To be kept in touch about Sherman Cymru events register for our e-bulletin online at **www.shermancymru.co.uk**

Sherman Cymru acknowledges the public investment of the Arts Council of Wales and Cardiff Council without whose support our work could not continue. Our Learning and Engagement work is currently supported by The Millennium Stadium Charitable Trust, Paul Hamlyn Foundation and The Rayne Foundation. Recent productions and projects have also been supported by Esmée Fairbairn Foundation, Oakdale Trust and The Peggy Ramsay Foundation.

CIARAN MCINTYRE
Des James

Theatre
Endgame, Port Authority (Liverpool Everyman); *Comedy of Errors, The Merry Wives of Windsor, Coriolanus, The Seagull, A Jovial Crew, All's Well That Ends Well* (Royal Shakespeare Company); *In Celebration* (Duke of York's Theatre) *Coriolanus, Under the Black Flag* (Shakespeare's Globe); *Richard II* (Old Vic Theatre); *The Quare Fellow* (Oxford Stage Company); *A Whistle in the Dark* (Citizens' Theatre, Glasgow); *The Lieutenant of Inishmore* (National Tour); *The Head of Red O'Brien* (Bewley's Cafe Theatre, Dublin); *The Fourth Wise Man* (Ark Theatre Company); *The Playboy of the Western World* (Leicester Haymarket Theatre); *Hard Times* (Storytellers, Dublin); *The Wedding* (Coventry Belgrade Theatre); *Dancing At Lughnasa* (Torch Theatre Company); *Reading Turgenev* (Meridian Theatre Company, Cork); *Waiting For Godot* (Contact Theatre Company); *The Weavers* (Gate Theatre Company); *Ethel Workman is Innocent* (Chelsea Centre Theatre); *The Hairy Ape* (Bristol Old Vic).

Television
The Time of Your Life (ITV); *Holby City, Inspector Lynley, Doctors, Comedy Nation, Absolutely Fabulous* (BBC Television); *Poliokoff 04* (Freemantle Media); *Birds of a Feather* (Alomo Productions)

Radio
The Old Tune, Talking in Whispers (BBC Radio); *Twilights* (BBC Radio Wales).

RHIAN MORGAN
Doreen James

Theatre
Includes: *The Importance of Being Earnest* (Mappa Mundi); *Cariad Mr Bustl/Le Misanthrope* (Theatr Genedlaethol Cymru); *Amazing Grace* (Wales Theatre Company); *Buzz* (Sgript Cymru); *Siwan* (Theatr Gwynedd); *Electra* (Chapter Arts & Dubrovnic Theatre Festival); *August* (Theatr Clwyd); *Hamlet, Miss Julie, Peer Gynt, A Doll's House* (Theatrig); *Macbeth* (Ways and Means).

Television
Includes: *Jennie – Y Daith Anorfod, Calon Gaeth, Rhian, Pobol y Cwm, A Mind to Kill* (S4C); *Eros Unleashed* (ITV Wales); *Mine All Mine* (ITV).

Film
The Black Dog (Midsummer Films); *August* (Granada Films). Rhian was nominated for a BAFTA Best Actress Award for her role in the film *August*.

Radio
Rhian has worked extensively for BBC Radio Drama and credits include: *Martha, Jac a Sianco* (Radio Cymru); *Ll Files* (Radio Wales); *After Life* (Radio 4).

ROBERT BOWMAN
Brian Cathcart /
Lieutenant Colonel Nigel Josling

Theatre

The Crucible, The Prisoner's Dilemma, Love In the Woods, The Comedy Of Errors, Twelfth Night, Wives Excuse, The Broken Heart (Royal Shakespeare Company); *The Odyssey* (Bristol Old Vic); *The Nest* (Living Pictures Productions); *Ivanov, The Oresteia, Haroun & The Sea Of Stories, An Inspector Calls* (Royal National Theatre); *Spinning Into Butter, (The Royal Court Theatre); As I Lay Dying, Twelfth Night, More Grimm Tales* (Young Vic Ensemble); *Grimm Tales* (International Tour); *King Lear* (West Yorkshire Playhouse).

As director theatre credits include: *Ghosts, The Seagull* (Bristol Old Vic); *The Blue Room* (Theatre Royal Bath); *Free From Sorrow, Andromache* (Living Pictures Productions); *The Seagull, A Small Family Business* (RWCMD).

Robert is Joint Artistic Director of Living Pictures Productions.

Television
Charles II, The Whistle Blower (BBC Television).

SIMON MOLLOY
Nicholas Blake QC

Theatre
Includes: *Humble Boy* (Royal Theatre, Northampton); *I Am Falling* (Gate Theatre); *The Representative* (Finborough Theatre); *Pillars of the Community, Love's Comedy* (National Theatre); *Beyond Belief, Pygmalion, Measure for Measure* (Manchester Library Theatre); *Twelfth Night* (Berengar Theatre); *Habeas Corpus* (Oldham Coliseum); *One For The Road* (Hampstead Theatre); *Duet for One* (Sheffield Crucible); *Educating Rita* (Leicester Haymarket); *Moving Pictures, The Genius* (Leeds Playhouse).

Television
Includes: *Poirot* (ITV); *Ashes to Ashes, Eastenders, Doctors, Silent Witness, Holby City, Casualty* (BBC Television); *Heartbeat/The Royal, The Innocents, A Day in Summer* (Yorkshire Television); *Baby War, Hillsborough* (Granada Television); *Wire in the Blood* (Tyne Tees); *Trust* (Box TV); *Clocking Off* (Red Productions); *Footballers' Wives* (Shed Productions).

Film
Heart (Granada Film); *Wilde* (Samuelson Ent); *Ladder of Swords* (Channel 4 Films).

Radio
Living With Betty (BBC Radio 2); *Morning Stories, Middlemarch* (BBC Radio 4).

ROBERT BLYTHE
Frank Swann / Bruce George MP

Theatre
Under Milk Wood, Mother Clap's Molly House, Henry V, Henry IV – parts 1 & 2 (National Theatre); *Badfinger* (Donmar Warehouse); *The Life of Galileo, Equus, The Norman Conquests, Entertaining Mr Sloane, Bedroom Farce, One Flew Over the Cuckoo's Nest, A Chorus of Disapproval, An Inspector Calls, The Cherry Orchard* (Clwyd Theatr Cymru); *House and Garden* (Stephen Joseph Theatre, Scarborough); *Ghosts* (The Royal Exchange Theatre, Manchester); *Macbeth, Educating Rita, No More Sitting on the Old School Bench, Dracula, Bull, Rock and Nut, In Sunshine and in Shadow, Crash Course, Season's Greetings* (Sherman Theatre Company).

Television
Includes: *The Brief, Little Britain, Doctors, The Bill, Waking the Dead, Without Motive, Casualty, Heartbeat, The Governor, The Famous Five, The Broker's Man, Delta Wave, The Biz, Preston Front, Middlemarch, Harri Webb, The Secret Life of Michael Fry, The Lifeboat, Eastenders, Coronation Street, Civvies, Minder, The Snow Spider, The Royal, Midsomer Murders, High Hopes (Series 1-6).*

Film
Includes: *Lie Still, The Theory of Flight, The Woodlanders, Darklands, The Englishman Who Went Up a Hill But Came Down a Mountain, The Love Child, Rebecca's Daughters, Whoops Apocalypse, And Nothing but the Truth, Experienced Preferred but Not Essential.*

RHIAN BLYTHE
Jonesy

Rhian Blythe trained at Queen Margaret University, Edinburgh.

Theatre
Romeo a Juliet, Plas Drycin, Hen Rebel, Dominos (Theatr Genedlaethol Cymru); *Bitsh* (Cwmni'r Frân Wen); *Porth y Byddar* (Theatr Genedlaethol Cymru/Clwyd Theatr Cymru); *Mae Gynno Ni Hawl Ar Y Ser* (Llwyfan Gogledd Cymru); *Blink* (F.A.B. Theatre).

Television
Mostyn Fflint 'n Aye (Teledu Elidir); *Talcen Caled* (Ffilmiau'r Nant); *Man Del* (Tonfedd Eryri).

Radio
Fire of the Dragon (BBC Radio Wales).

Rhian would like to thank Jo 'Jonesy' for all her help.

PHILIP RALPH
Writer

Philip Ralph is a writer and performer. He trained at the Royal Academy of Dramatic Art and has worked extensively in theatre and television for the last sixteen years.

Theatre
He was a writer on attachment at Soho Theatre in 2002 and his first play, *Mr Nobody*, premiered at Soho in 2003. His second play, *Hitting Funny*, (a one-man show in which he performed) was produced by Volcano Theatre Company. He was nominated for Best Actor at the Stage Awards in Edinburgh, 2005, for his performance in *Hitting Funny*.

Television
In addition to his stage writing, he is a regular writer for the BBC Television daytime drama, *Doctors*.

MICK GORDON
Director

Mick Gordon is Artistic Director of On Theatre and On Film and Head of Directing at East 15. He was Trevor Nunn's Associate Director at the Royal National Theatre and was Director of the National's *Transformation* Season. Previously he was Artistic Director of London's Gate Theatre.

Theatre
As writer and director credits include: *On Emotion* and *On Ego* with Paul Broks (Soho Theatre); On *Religion* with AC Grayling (Soho Theatre; Europalia Festival Belgium; Lucille Lortel Theatre, New York; BBC Radio 4); *On Love in Uzbekistan* (Ilhom Theatre, Tashkent); *On Love* (Gate Theatre; BBC Radio4); *On Death* with Marie de Hennezel (Gate Theatre & Wellcome Collection).

As director theatre credits include: *Grimms Tales* (Dusko Radovic, Belgrade); *Dancing at Lughnasa* (Lyric Theatre, Belfast); *Optic Trilogy, A Play in Swedish, English and Italian* (Dramatan Theatre, Stockholm); *War, Lovers, The Real Thing, Betrayal* (Strindberg Theatre, Stockholm); *A Prayer for Owen Meany, The Walls, Le Pub!* (National Theatre); *Monkey!* (Young Vic); *Trust* (Royal Court); *Salome* (Riverside Studios); *Godspell* (Chichester Festival Theatre); *My Fair Lady, Closer, Art* (National Theatre, Buenos Aires); *Volunteers, Marathon, Une Tempete* (Gate Theatre); *Measure for Measure* (English Touring Theatre); *Hamlet, The Tales of Hoffman* (National Theatre Studio); *Renard* (National Youth Ballet); *The Promise, Arabian Nights* (BAC); *The Soldier's Tale* (Institut Francais).

IGOR VASILJEV
Designer

Igor Vasiljev was born in Pula and graduated from the Scenography Department of the Academy of Applied Arts in Belgrade.

Theatre
Recent production credits include: *Grimms Tales* (directed by Mick Gordon); *Mozart Luster Lustik* (directed by Jay Scheib); *Gespensterhaus* (directed by Thierry Bruehl, at the Taschenoper Festival, Salzburg); *Waiting for Godot, Blasted, Three Sisters* (directed by Đurđa Tešić); *The Cherry Orchard* (directed by Predrag Kalaba); *Romance, The Face of Glass* (directed by Anja Suša); *Prometheus Bound* (directed by Stevan Bodroža); *Orpheus and Eurydice* (directed by Bojana Cvejić).

His work also explores the field of digital media (digital art, photography, electro-acoustic music) and he is professionally involved in video and graphic/web design.

He was awarded the Theatre Prize at the YUSTAT Biennale of Stage Design and Annual Duško Radović in Belgrade and he has exhibited at the Prague Quadrinnale.

ANDREW JONES
Lighting Designer

Theatre
Andrew was Co-artistic Director of the award-winning Volcano Theatre Company between 1987 and 1998. Andrew was also responsible for the lighting, set and costume design, and technical management of the 21 shows produced by the company during that time, which included *L.O.V.E.*, *How To Live, Manifesto, After The Orgy* and *Macbeth – The Director's Cut.*

Andrew has been Production Manager on numerous international tours by major UK companies including the National Theatre, the Akram Khan Company, the Michael Clark Company and Random Dance.

Andrew is currently a specialist Drama and Dance Adviser for the British Council, where his role revolves around the development and delivery of innovative performance, collaborative and education programmes in 33 countries within the former Soviet Bloc, Scandinavia and Central Asia

Continuing to work as a freelance lighting designer, this is Andrew's first collaboration with Mick Gordon and Sherman Cymru.

MIKE FURNESS
Sound Designer

Mike has worked on a number of
theatre projects over the last few years.
He also produces talking books and
designs sound systems for a broad
range of live events worldwide.

Theatre
Sound Designs in 2007/8 include:
The Changeling (ETT / Nottingham
Playhouse); *Lyrical M.C.* (Tamasha);
Fantastic Mr Fox (Open Air Theatre,
Regents Park); *A Fine Balance*
(Hampstead Theatre); *Child of The
Divide* (Tamasha US Tour); *Someone
Else's Shoes* (Soho Theatre).

Other productions include: *All's Well
That Ends Well, As You Like It* (RSC);
Mother Courage (National Theatre);
*Blues In The Night, The Witches,
Ladyday, The BFG* (West End); *The
Trouble With Asian Men, On Religion*
(On Theatre); *The Manchurian
Candidate* (Lyric Hammersmith); and
productions for: The Tricycle, Paines
Plough, Bristol Old Vic, Birmingham
Rep, West Yorkshire Playhouse and
the Edinburgh, Brighton and Salisbury
Festivals.

JULIANE VON SIVERS
Assistant Director

Originally from Halle in Germany,
Juliane is currently enrolled on the
MFA Theatre Directing course at East
15.

Theatre
Assistant Director credits include: *The
Idiots* (Pan Pan at the Dublin Theatre
Festival); *Urban Poems* (Guna Nua,
Dublin).

In addition to completing an internship
at the Central School of Speech
and Drama, she has presented the
interactive play *Börse des Wissens* at
the International Summer School in
Halle, and has worked as assistant to
the director at the Thalia Theatre in
Halle.

BRENDA KNIGHT
Company Stage Manager

Brenda trained in Stage Management at the Welsh College of Music and Drama.

Theatre
Brenda has worked all over the country with such illustrious companies as Sherman Cymru, Hijinx, Theatr Clwyd, Theatre Centre, Wales Theatre Company and Excalibur Productions.

She is a founder member of Mappa Mundi Theatre Company, who will be touring their popular production of *Canterbury Tales* around the UK this Autumn.

NATASHA WHITE
Deputy Stage Manager

Natasha gained a Postgraduate Diploma in Stage Management from the Royal Welsh College of Music and Drama.

Theatre
Natasha worked as Assistant Stage Manager on the Sherman Theatre Company Christmas production of *The Stories of Hans Christian Andersen* and on last year's Sherman Cymru Christmas production, *Beauty and the Beast*. She was also Stage Manager for the Spring Acting Out Cardiff production, *Belong÷Division*. Other companies she has worked for include Hijinx Theatre Company, Mappa Mundi, Creation Theatre, 3BUGS, Bridge House Theatre Company, Cwmni Inc and Mess Up The Mess.

She has recently started working as a freelance UK and Overseas Expedition and Team Leader for World Challenge.

DEEP CUT

First published in 2008 by Oberon Books Ltd
521 Caledonian Road, London N7 9RH
Tel: 020 7607 3637 / Fax: 020 7607 3629
e-mail: info@oberonbooks.com
www.oberonbooks.com

A catalogue record for this book is available from the British
Library.

ISBN: 978-1-84002-874-4

Cover image by Kirsten McTernan

Printed in Great Britain by CPI Antony Rowe, Chippenham.

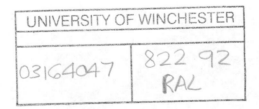

Four young people lost their lives at Deepcut. Four families grieve for them.

This play focuses on just one of these families but this should not be taken to imply that the James's story is considered to be in any way superior, more important or more worthy of telling. On the contrary, it is hoped that they might be seen simply as representative of all such families who have lost loved ones in the armed forces in circumstances that are less than transparent.

This play is dedicated to the memory of PTE SEAN BENTON, PTE CHERYL JAMES, PTE GEOFF GRAY and PTE JAMES COLLINSON and to their families and loved ones who continue to fight for answers, justice and closure.

Contents

Author's note

In January 2008 the Armed Forces Minister, Bob Ainsworth MP, announced that Deepcut barracks in Surrey would be closing in 2013 and its land would be sold off for residential development. This was said to be unrelated to the four deaths that had occurred there between 1995 and 2002 – although the families of the four recruits were notified of the closure – but was simply part of ongoing re-assessment of army training. Press reaction was desultory at best – a few interviews with the parents, the odd article – and within 24 hours the news cycle had moved on. And why should it not have done? Deepcut, after all, was very old news. If anything, the announcement of the closure was seen simply as the last word on a story that was long since over.

I was commissioned to write this play by the late Sgript Cymru in December 2005. The initial brief was extremely broad – I think the original question posed by artistic director Simon Harris was: 'Would you be interested in writing a play about the army? Women in the army? Iraq? Deepcut?' The Deepcut story was still in the press at the time as the publication of the Blake Review was imminent. I discovered that, of the four recruits who died, the only woman was Welsh. I live and work in Wales so this was my starting point. I went back to the company and said that I would like to write about the army's duty of care to its recruits and I would begin by approaching the family of Cheryl James to see if they would talk to me. I also said at that fateful meeting that I thought it should be a verbatim play – a decision I will come back to later. I composed an extremely carefully worded letter to Cheryl's parents, posted it and waited. A few months passed and I'd heard nothing. Deepcut clearly wouldn't be part of my story. Then a week or so after the Blake Review was published I received a telephone call from Des James saying he would be interested in meeting with me. I had absolutely no idea what I was getting myself into.

Over the next two and a half years whenever anyone would ask me what I was working on, almost without exception, the following conversation would take place:

ME: 'I'm working on a play about the deaths at Deepcut army barracks.'

ANYONE: 'Oh, isn't that where the army said they were suicides but they were actually murdered and it was covered up?'

This reaction is not in itself shocking other than in its absolute lack of surprise or concern. Most people that I speak to about Deepcut seem to have resigned themselves to the belief that some form of conspiracy or cover-up has taken place surrounding these deaths but – heigh-ho – that's just the way of the world. If we were to concern ourselves with every instance of alleged corruption within the state, we would have no time left in which to live our lives. And, after all, what can we really do about it? Whilst this is a sad and common fact of life, this attitude does beg the question – if the broadly accepted opinion is that these four deaths were not suicides, then why has the story been allowed to simply fade away with the key questions left unanswered? Namely – how did they die and why?

The state – and by that I mean the government, the MoD, the police, the army and the judiciary – would strongly argue that these questions *have* been answered. The four deaths were tragic suicides and this has been conclusively proven:

- Surrey Police, accepting that its initial investigations were flawed, conducted a rigorous and extensive re-investigation into all four deaths and concluded that there was no evidence to suggest any third party involvement or any prospect of a prosecution relating to the deaths;
- Surrey's investigations were reviewed by Devon and Cornwall police who – with a few reservations – declared them to be sound;
- The House of Commons Defence Select Committee (HCDSC) carried out an inquiry into duty of care in the armed forces and concluded that there were significant problems but that they were being rectified;
- The Adult Learning Inspectorate (ALI) conducted an inspection and assessment of all army training establishments and recommended improvements;
- And finally, Nicholas Blake QC, a respected human rights lawyer, reviewed the existing evidence on the four deaths and concluded that 'on the balance of probabilities' all four were suicides and there was little or no connection to bullying or abuse.

So, they were four tragic suicides which had brought to light systemic failures within the army that had been rectified. The story is, rightly, over.

However, there is another side to this story – as the families of those who died and their representatives would argue:

- Surrey police's initial investigations were not simply flawed but inept to the point of incompetence or worse; their re-investigations were arguably inadequate, allegedly corrupt and the reports from these investigations have never been made available to the families;

- Devon and Cornwall's review into Surrey police raised serious concerns with regard to 'mindset' issues – e.g. Surrey's alleged aim was not to investigate possible foul play but simply to re-prove suicide – alongside the assertion that Surrey should have treated the deaths as murders from the outset. However the Devon & Cornwall report was not made public and none of the complaints made against Surrey police by the families were upheld by the Independent Police Complaints Commission;
- The HCDSC inquiry wasn't into Deepcut nor did it seek to answer the question of how the recruits died;
- Similarly the ALI report had nothing to do with the deaths but addressed itself to training practices and conditions;
- And finally, Nicholas Blake's review had no power to compel or cross examine witnesses, was only able to review existing evidence (unavailable to the families) from the disputed Surrey investigation, revealed a catalogue of allegations of abuse and bullying and yet concluded that 'on the balance of probabilities' the deaths were suicides – the 'balance of probabilities' being a legal phrase meaning more than 51% certainty which is a very long way from 'beyond all reasonable doubt'.

Unsurprisingly, the families maintain their call for an independent public inquiry and argue that the story is very far from being over.

So, whilst there are arguments on both sides, what is clear is that *how* these four young people died has never been conclusively addressed; and it logically follows that *why* they died has also never been conclusively addressed. So, why the story has been allowed to fade away with these questions left unanswered is anybody's guess.

But why does it matter? After all, people die in the armed forces every day. It's part of the job, an accepted risk, life in the army's tough, if you can't stand the heat, etc, etc. Why should the deaths of these four young people, tragic though they were, be given so much attention and concern? And why should they be the subject of a play?

It matters, I would argue, because the story of Deepcut represents a sickness at the heart of our society. These young people signed up willingly to an institution that should be one of the backbones of our society; the army represents – whatever ones feelings towards war and conflict – safety, stability, and strength. We are often told, by government and media alike, that we have 'the best army in the world'. Regardless of who these young people were – mere privates in the army's supply regiment – no stone should have been left unturned to discover the exact circumstances behind their deaths and, once discovered, those responsible should have been held to account and every step taken to prevent the reoccurrence of such events. But none of this happened. The families have been met with misdirection, confusion, lies and disdain. The deaths at Deepcut represent a low water mark in relations between the state and the public; a massive failure of transparency and account-ability; and a demonstration that public suspicion towards the state is, not only justified, but necessary.

The army is at one of the lowest points in its history. Recruitment and investment are at an all-time low, wastage (trained personnel leaving the service) at an all-time high, and all this at a time when they are heavily committed in multiple conflicts overseas. (Indeed, arguably, it is no coincidence that the full repercussions of the Deepcut deaths were so successfully 'avoided' by the state, since the story broke in the media in 2002 when the army were already involved in Afghanistan and conflict in Iraq was looming. Hardly the best time to be facing accusations of institutional failure and collapse...) The families are often accused of being 'anti-army' and, I'm sure, this play will receive the same accusa-tion. Nothing could be further from the truth. In reality the position of the families and the agenda behind this play is, I believe, profoundly 'pro-army'. *The army should be better than this.* Its recruits – whatever their regiment, whatever their background – should be treated with the utmost care and concern. They do an incredibly difficult, dangerous job and receive precious little by way of reward or gratitude. Young people should *want* to join the army, fully aware of the risks, because it is a fantastic job and life opportunity and not because they feel like they have no other choice or have been hoodwinked into believing it is something it is not.

The army would argue that it has put its house in order as a result of Deepcut and such things could never happen again. And yet I recently was made aware of a young person who was incorrectly placed in an infantry unit, despite being recruited to intelligence, attempted to transfer but was ignored for over a year, was bullied and abused, both mentally and physically, and was eventually forced to go AWOL and face a court martial. After five years, this person is still fighting to get out of the army, despite serious concerns for their mental and physical wellbeing. And this is just one example of many. The army is a public service and we as taxpayers should be sure that, despite its famous secrecy and the sacrosanct nature of the chain of command, it is being run and operated in a way which cares for and respects the young men and women who enter the service. But, as Amnesty International point out, UK army service remains, in effect, 'bonded servitude' with no redress for grievances outside the chain of command and absolutely no independent representation.

But no institution emerges untainted by Deepcut. Not the police, the government or the judiciary. And this is why it matters. Transparency and accountability should be the watchwords of our state institutions yet all too often they are treated as some kind of naïve idealist's joke. And there is another institution that has been tainted by this story too: the press – and who'd have believed that their reputation could be any more besmirched? The myth that the press has the ability to hold the state to account has been shattered irrevocably by Deepcut (as Brian Cathcart elucidates in Appendix B2, page 107). This is a complex, multi-layered and bewildering story that the press – with a few notable exceptions – has been singularly unable to encompass and communicate, other than via lurid headlines or repeated government soundbites. And just when it became apparent that the state was unable or unwilling to provide conclusive answers, the press then dropped the story for reasons known only to them – 'compassion fatigue', perhaps. As a result, the state was able to easily avoid some of the glaring discrepancies and holes in its story and thereby escape the full glare of public attention and concern.

So, why should this be the subject of a play? Is it not best left to *Panorama* or some such TV documentary? I would argue that this story represents exactly what theatre should be about, what it should be doing. Theatre, in my opinion, is a forum for debate via story. A place where we look at our society, hold it up to the light and examine its flaws and beauties – and they are writ large in the story of Deepcut. Theatre is a place where we should ask questions of ourselves – What kind of an army do we want? What do we want the press to do? How much transparency and accountability do we believe the state should practice? Do we want something like Deepcut to be going on right under our noses and do nothing about it? I believe that this is a vital story of our times that we should not ignore and I believe the theatre is the place to tell it. The counter-argument that has often been made to me is that the story has no ending: we still don't know how they died. And my argument has remained the same: that *is* the story. The James and the other families have to face spending the rest of their lives without ever knowing the full facts of how their children died and the question we have to ask ourselves is simple: why?

And why verbatim? There has been an explosion in this form of theatre in the past ten years. Indeed, under New Labour, verbatim theatre has flourished. (Could there be a connection, I wonder? A famously controlling and spin-obsessed government going hand in hand with a form of theatre in which audiences perceive that they are getting at some kind of hidden 'truth'?) And as verbatim has flourished and become dominant in so-called 'political' theatre, so the argument has arisen that somehow it has passed its sell-by date. We've had enough now. There's too much verbatim. The form is tired and old. Naturally,

I would argue to the contrary – indeed, I believe that it is at times like this that a re-evaluation of the form is called for, not simply its dismissal. Verbatim is not 'truth'. It is resolutely mediated speech; otherwise I would be unable to take a writer's credit. But it is certainly as close as we are going to get in the theatre to the 'truth', (whatever that may be) especially when dealing with actual events. I was certain at the beginning of this process (and I am even more so now) that in order to tell a story so full of confusion, misdirection and unknowns, the only way to do so would be via verbatim. To begin to 'adapt' the words of those I interviewed or to 'dramatise' events that I was not present at would be disingenuous at best, and leave the play wide open to accusations of inaccuracy and manipulation of the facts at worst. So, in every respect, the story itself dictated the form in which it should be told. I believe there is no better way to tell this particular story than via verbatim theatre.

But there are as many forms of 'verbatim' as there are writers of verbatim plays. This particular play has been constructed from transcripts of interviews that I conducted alongside extracts from journalism, the Blake Review and Hansard among other sources; the intention being to place the James's personal, private story squarely within the context of state and journalistic response – a position which has been largely denied to them except on the limited occasions when the press were interested. It should be stated, however, that at no time did I approach a member of the serving army, government or MoD for an interview or comment and this, of course, leads to the accusation that the play is nothing more than a one-sided polemic. My argument against this is simple: the government and the MoD have daily, unfettered access to the loudest possible megaphone – namely, the UK press – and they have used it to make their case consistently and at length for over six years. If, for 90 minutes, I can go some way to provide this family and others with access to a megaphone of their own then I see that as being absolutely the right course of action and I make no apology for it. But, ultimately, what would be the point of approaching the MoD? If it takes Des James, whose daughter died in the MoD's care, *three months* to receive a non-committal reply to a letter querying the manner of her death, then why on earth would I, a mere writer, attempt to make contact with such an organisation who would undoubtedly take far longer to respond with an inevitable 'no comment'?

So, make no mistake, the story of Deepcut is not over. In fact, the announcement of the closure only re-proves that point. It is not over for the families whose struggle for a public inquiry goes on; it should not be over for the press who, as Brian Cathcart puts it, have 'dropped the ball'; it is not over for today's recruits into the army, many of whom, we learn daily, face the same issues and problems as Sean, Cheryl, Geoff and James. And it should not be over for you, the reader or viewer of this play. The story of Deepcut is the story of your army, your government and your country. And we all deserve better.

Working on this project has been the most extraordinarily rewarding time of my life. There are many people to thank and I do so at length in the acknowledgements section. But I would like to take this opportunity to thank Des and Doreen James for their openness, warmth, honesty and willingness to participate in this process, even when it looked as though the play would never see the light of day. It has been an enormous privilege and I hope that this play helps in some small way to bring them peace.

Philip Ralph, June 2008

Acknowledgements

Any play is a collaborative effort but a project such as this requires the culmination of work by many, many individuals – especially since it has been well over two years since it was first commissioned. The following list is as exhaustive as I could make it but, inevitably, there may be someone I have omitted to mention for which I apologise.

I would like to offer my heartfelt thanks (in roughly chronological order) to:

Simon Harris: who asked the first fateful question, survived my driving (though he never lets me live it down!) and has been a constant support from the first moment to the last.

Emma Goad: my 'Harper Lee', who shared many hours on the road and in interviews and who, in the time it has taken me to write this play, has got married and started a family!

Arwel Gruffydd and Elen Bowman: who have undoubtedly been this play's fairy godmothers – without them the difficult transition from one company to the next and the drive to see it produced would most probably never have happened.

The staff of Sgript Cymru: Mai Jones, Branwen Davies and Carys Shannon for their unstinting support and enthusiasm for the project.

Robin Soans: for his invaluable advice.

All those people I interviewed who gave their time freely: Des and Doreen James, Jonesy, Frank Swann and Brian Cathcart whose words are in the play – but also to those who, unfortunately, there was not enough space to include: Kirsty, Livio Zilli from Amnesty International, Major (Retd.) Eccles, Lembit Opik MP, Richard Norton-Taylor, Robert Fox and William Bache.

I would also like to especially thank Anwen Humphreys and Keith Johnson whom I interviewed very early on in the process. They both suffer from Gulf War Syndrome and campaign for justice, recognition and compensation from the MoD and government. This is a cause that clearly deserves more support from the general public and I am deeply sorry that the play was unable to encompass it. More information about the campaign can be found via the National Gulf Families and Veterans Association: www.ngvfa.com.

Chris Ricketts and all the staff at Sherman Cymru: Sian Summers, Kate Perridge, Haleh Tozer, Suzanne Carter, Jenny Boyatt, Elin Partridge and everyone who has worked so incredibly hard on the production and made it possible.

Mick Gordon who has been the most wonderful collaborator and friend throughout the difficult process of taking a five-hour script and turning it into a 90-minute one and whose ideas, support, enthusiasm and creativity have been, and continue to be, extraordinary.

James Hogan and all the staff at Oberon books for being bold enough to agree to publish. And for the lovely shepherd's pie...

BBC Radio 5 Live Breakfast with Nicky Campbell for kindly allowing the use of the interview with Des James.

Heather Mills and Sheila Molnar at *Private Eye* magazine for allowing use and publication of their superb article.

All the actors who took part in the workshop week for their help, feedback, enthusiasm and patience: Dan Curtis, Joanna Griffiths, Robin Hooper, Adam James, Rhydian Jones, Michelle Luther and Ian Redford.

The actors in the production for their dedication and tireless hard work – Rhian Blythe, Robert Blythe, Robert Bowman, Ciaran McIntyre, Simon Molloy and Rhian Morgan.

Igor Vasiljev, Andrew Jones, Mike Furness and the technical and stage management departments of Sherman Cymru and the Traverse for creating the amazing physical world of the play and working so hard to realise it so brilliantly.

Lee Haven-Jones and Dewi Gregory from Truth Department.

Dominic Hill, Katherine Mendelsohn and all at the Traverse for agreeing to present the play during their festival season and for all their support and valuable feedback.

My agent, Julia Tyrrell, for her constant, unfailing support.

My friends who have read the play and given me invaluable feedback: Jack Blumenau, Simon Robson, Christopher Megson, Mike Ward, Meredydd Barker and Michael Dawson.

My partner, Fern – for everything.

Part 1: The Play

List of sources

Source notations appear at the end of relevant sections and can encompass several lines of text from several different speakers. [ ] within text denotes additions or elisions by the author for purposes of clarity or clarification. No attempt whatsoever has been made to alter meanings or inferences. Text denoted in such a way is either the product of the author's imagination or based directly upon verbatim transcripts. All other text is sourced. The text is accurate to the first week of rehearsals. Any changes thereafter have been cuts to, or re-arrangements of, the material included in the published text.

[V] – Verbatim transcripts derived from interviews with the author.

The Deepcut Review & Nicholas Blake QC

© Parliamentary Copyright 2006. The text of this Report may be reproduced in whole or in part free of charge in any format or media without requiring specific permission. This is subject to the material not being used in a derogatory manner or in a misleading context. Where the material is being republished or copied to others, the source of the material must be identified and the copyright status acknowledged.

The Deepcut Review is available to view and download from the MoD's website:
www.MoD.uk/DefenceInternet/AboutDefence/CorporatePublications/
PersonnelPublications/DutyofCare/DeepcutReview.htm

N.B. Sergeant B as referred to in this play is the Sergeant B of the Deepcut Review. However, Private A and Private B have been changed for reasons of narrative expediency. They represent, respectively, Private AA and Private AB as referred to in Chapter 6 of the Review.

[B1] – Nicholas Blake QC's press statement on publication of the 'Deepcut Review', 29th March 2006.
[B2] – Deepcut Review, Appendix 3: correspondence between Frank Swann and Nicholas Blake, QC.
[B3] – Deepcut Review, Chapter 6: The Death of Cheryl James, Nicholas Blake QC.
[B4] – Deepcut Review, Chapter 5: The Death of Sean Benton, Nicholas Blake QC.
[B5] – Deepcut Review, Chapter 10: The Death of Geoff Gray, Nicholas Blake QC.

[B6] – Nicholas Blake's press statement on announcement of the 'Deepcut Review', 15th December 2004.

[B7] – Deepcut Review, Appendix 4/8: Meeting with Mr & Mrs James and Colonel Josling.

[B8] – Deepcut Review, Press Briefing, 29th March 2006.

Journalism

[J1] – *Private Eye* report published 15th September 2006 – 'Deepcut: Shots In The Dark', written by Heather Mills and Brian Cathcart. Used with kind permission of the authors and *Private Eye* magazine. Reproduced in full in Appendix B1 (pp 88–106).

[J2] – *British Journalism Review*, Volume 18, No. 1, 2007 – 'A Case of Journalism Outmanoeuvred', written by Brian Cathcart. Used with kind permission of the author. Reproduced in full in Appendix B2 (pp 107–11).

[J3] – Independent article published 29th July 2004 – 'What really happened at Deepcut barracks?' Written by Brian Cathcart. Used with kind permission of the author.

[J4] – BBC Wales TV interview, 29th March 2006.

[J5] – North West Evening Mail, 10th August 2005.

[J6] – BBC News Reports and websites.

Establishment debates, reports and statements

[E1] – Surrey Police Press Statements.

[E2] – Press release from Independent Police Complaints Commission, 11/07/06.

[E3] – House of Commons Defence Select Committee's third report of session 2004–05, on Duty of Care. (Includes use of Minutes of Evidence.)

[E4] – Hansard.

Miscellaneous (private and other sources)

[O1] – 'Deepcut & Beyond' website.

[O2] – Eulogy for Cheryl James written by Des James. Used with kind permission.

Characters
(in order of appearance)

DES JAMES
Father of Cheryl James who died at Deepcut
barracks in 1995

DOREEN JAMES
Cheryl's mother and Des's wife

BRIAN CATHCART
Journalist

NICHOLAS BLAKE QC
Human rights lawyer and author of the
Deepcut Review

FRANK SWANN
Independent Forensics Expert

JONESY
Contemporary recruit of Cheryl James's
at Deepcut

BRUCE GEORGE MP
Chair of Defence Select Committee

LIEUTENANT COLONEL NIGEL JOSLING
Commanding Officer at Deepcut in 1995

Doubling:
FRANK SWANN / BRUCE GEORGE
BRIAN CATHCART / NIGEL JOSLING

Act One

The home of DES and DOREEN JAMES.

As the audience enter, the radio plays an interview between Des James and Nicky Campbell of Radio Five Live's Breakfast show, discussing the implications of the closure of Deepcut which aired in January 2008. As this ends, house lights down.

Lights up.

DES JAMES – informally dressed – is sitting listening to an excerpt from the above interview. After a minute he stands, turns off the radio and addresses the audience.

DES: [Quite some time ago now] our legal counsel made a formal application for a public inquiry to the Secretary of State since they believe that the Blake report has strengthened the case for a public inquiry but the protocol is that you have to make that application for it to be refused. Ironically. When it is refused, you can then apply for a judicial review of that decision, the decision to refuse, if you applied for a judicial review for a public inquiry they would come back and say, 'Well, it hasn't been refused', you know? [Anyway, the Armed Forces Minister at the time of Blake offered the families a meeting to discuss the case and I've now taken that up with his successor, but he's refusing to honour that offer. He says he doesn't believe such a meeting would serve any useful purpose and that 'There is no public or service interest in pursuing a public inquiry' – which is preposterous when no one knows what actually happened and no one has ever been held accountable for the… (*Beat.*) Sorry, I'm probably not making much sense, am I? Getting ahead of myself.] Can I just grab a coffee? [I'm sure Doreen will be along to speak to you later,] to be honest with you.

He gets a coffee and sits.

Getting back to… [Doreen and I] were married in '71. Probably around, I guess, '77, '78, we finally accepted that we weren't going to have kids of our own. In those days you actually went to the local church, the local vicar and the Church of England did a lot of this stuff then and…it was different, you know. And we had visits from social workers and you're sort of being vetted, which was fine, I mean, I had a good job, Doreen, my wife's a nurse, y'know, there was really no issues there and…

Enter DOREEN JAMES, stylishly dressed, reserved, watchful.

DOREEN: [Sorry, excuse me.] This keeps ringing, Des, your phone –

DES: Who is it?

DOREEN: I don't know. I haven't answered it.

DES: Who is it, sorry?

DOREEN: It keeps ringing.

DES: Oh, right, no problem. There's not much point here. The reception is awful. [So, anyway, we…] Sorry, I've lost it just now, I'll think – when we – no, I've lost it.

DOREEN: Sorry, it's me, isn't it? Fussing about. I'll go now.

Exit DOREEN.

DES: What was I going to say? Yeah, that's right. Eventually [we had] Cheryl and her natural brother in January '79 and I mean the excitement when we brought the two of them home. Everything was fine, you know. Everything was fine.

As DES takes a drink of coffee, enter BRIAN CATHCART carrying boxes, files and notebooks which he gratefully puts down within the walls of the James's home and addresses the audience.

CATHCART: One of the reasons I'm a journalist is because of Watergate. When the scandal broke and the burglars were arrested and the first connections were made with the White House, the Justice Department initiated an investigation. The Attorney General went on television and [said] 'This has been one of the most exhaustive investigations ever undertaken by the Department and I can tell you that there was no connection with the White House'.

DES: When it first started most people in the press, certainly in the serious press, knew far more about it than I did. And then it's very strange because you go past that point. In fact even today I have reporters talking to me who don't know anything…and that's quite frustrating because you really have to understand what's gone on, otherwise you don't understand the implication of what's going on currently. [V]

Enter NICHOLAS BLAKE QC who uses the fridge as a lectern and begins to speak.

BLAKE: I welcome you all to this event marking the publication of my report. I am sorry there is so much to absorb in such a short space of time. A single headline cannot do justice to four separate events occurring between June 1995 and March 2002. In order to review the circumstances surrounding the deaths and the Army's response to them, it was first necessary to see if any conclusions could be reached on how each trainee died…
[B1]

CATHCART: [On 29th March 2006, Nicholas Blake QC, a respected human rights lawyer, published his review into the circumstances surrounding the deaths of four soldiers.]

Exit CATHCART.

DES: I think that you have to be careful, you know, I think that when you lose anyone there is a danger – well, not a danger but there's always an element that when you tell people about that person you embellish it a little. Not intentionally but you do – you forget all about the bad bits and you sort of, you know, you put a halo on them. And I'm very wary of that but I mean… I mean she was just a joy, you know I can't… I can't.. I can't tell you…sorry. [V]

35

BLAKE. Cheryl James died on lone guard duty. She had personal problems in her private life to resolve. There is an absence of any reason why this popular young woman would be the subject of attack and a complete absence of any evidence of any sort undermining the more probable hypothesis of self-harm. [B1]

DES: Sorry. No, it was erm she was a joy, that's all I can tell you. She was always highly competitive, always the joker, tomboy – there was a devilment, a mischief-ness – this person who giggles, was loud, smiling, laughing, joking… (*Beat.*) Christmas was the most special – I absolutely love Christmas, I'm like a kid, even today – and so you know we used to build up to it. We used to have trial runs in September. It's the truth, Doreen'll tell you. I used to [say] – 'Now, let me check, don't go in there whatever you do'. So, the two of them used to come on Christmas morning, you know, and they'd whisper in your ear, 'Are you going to check yet? Will you go and check now, Dad?' It'd be bloody four o'clock, you know. So, I'd go in and put the lights on the Christmas tree and I'd put the music on and just get the ambience and then I'd say, 'Ah, I think he's been. You can come in.' I used to put a tape recorder on. I've still got the tapes. I tried…that's one place I can't go, you know, I tried last Christmas, you know, I tried but…can't do that. [V]

BLAKE: At one point it was thought that independent scientific expertise might point away from a conclusion of self-inflicted death. Although Mr Frank Swann declined to make his opinions available to the Review – [B1]

Enter FRANK SWANN – direct, blunt – smartly dressed, wearing distinctive gold jewellery and carrying a mass of equipment – slide projector, roll up screen, boxes of slides, files etc.

SWANN: I have said from the very beginning of my forensic investigation that nothing less than a Judicial Public Inquiry into these four deaths will do and my decision is based solely on your lack of powers to compel witnesses.

BLAKE: My inability to compel witnesses does not prevent the evaluation of your forensic reports.

SWANN: If I can help you in any way, I shall, so long as it serves justice.

BLAKE: I know the families are anxious to achieve both justice and closure. If you can assist the review, I hope you will do so.

SWANN: After spending six weeks conducting a serious forensic study and tests, I have no intention of letting the MoD and the Government 'walk away' from the injustice of [these] ALLEGED 'suicides' of young recruits, which I am satisfied, were in fact MURDER[S]. **[B2]**

Exit SWANN.

DES: When Cheryl would have been 14, 15 at the end of that year and erm my sister's youngest son – now, we're going to...we're going to get through this – but this is very difficult for me. My sister's youngest child was a boy, he was 18. He and Cheryl were very, very close. She clearly loved him. He was a bit of a hero, you know? (*Beat.*) He committed suicide. 15th December '92. I can remember Cheryl telling me, she said, 'Christmas will never be the same again.' And so '93 was not a good year. **[V]**

BLAKE: Mr and Mrs James have pointed out to this Review that Cheryl was aware of the heartache and grief [the death of her cousin] caused the family and this was one reason why they believed Cheryl would never seek to inflict similar pain on anyone else. It has further come to light that 22 days after the suicide of the cousin, Cheryl herself was admitted to hospital following an overdose of paracetamol. Cheryl's Medical History Questionnaire was, thus, inaccurate in respect of previous self-harm attempts. **[B3]**

DES: It [sounds] as though she was on a stomach pump, doesn't it? Cheryl's 'self harm' was going to school and telling her friend that she'd taken some Panadol. Five –

three or five, I'm not sure. Her friend told the teacher, the teacher invoked policy, sent her to the hospital, the hospital called me, I went from work, she drank loads of water which is what they told her, and they sent her home. End of story. **[V]**

BLAKE: [Cheryl James] left school [in] the summer [of 1994] with three GCSE passes and started to study for A-levels, but did not find it was the right thing for her. There had been some adolescent tension resulting in Social Services' involvement and Cheryl leaving home. **[B3]**

DES: Came home one day, she'd just gone, didn't know where she was. It was all about – 'I want to be on my own, I don't want any rules and don't tell me' – and looking back it was all related to grief and my failure to even recognise it. I was so engrossed in my own grief – you know, I should have stepped up and done more...

Enter JONESY, in full RLC parade uniform. She marches in and stands to attention before standing easy.

JONESY: I do believe that everyone who goes in the Army [has] got a reason. Passed my GCSEs and did an A-level. I liked school. But I got in with – well, it wasn't the wrong crowd, we were just a bit loud, I suppose, and we got into fights and we got into a really bad fight one night. We ended up in court and it caused horrendous arguments at home. (*Beat.*) I was just standing there thinking 'My God, I just don't want to end up doing this', you know? 'Cause I knew I wasn't stupid, I'd done my education. And I didn't want to go to university. My mum and stepdad couldn't have afforded [it] anyway. I just didn't know what I wanted to do. **[V]**

DES: [This is Jonesy.

JONESY: My surname's Jones so that's what everyone in the Army used to call me.

DES: She was with Cheryl in the Army.]

JONESY: I mean, we were never best, best mates, don't get me wrong, you know, we weren't. But we always spoke and we always had a laugh. I saw her every day for six months, you know, brushed my teeth at the side of her, argued over the last bit of manky green stuff you wipe your hands on – just stupid things like that. [V]

Enter DOREEN who sits close to DES.

DES: [This is my wife, Doreen. I told you she'd speak to you.]

DOREEN: Well, it's on the day. Some days you can do it, other days you can't.

DOREEN hands DES a bottle of water.

DOREEN: Cause you're probably dry after talking.

DES: [Oh, thanks. So,] what happened was [Cheryl] wanted to go into the Air Force.

DOREEN: It was the Navy originally, but she didn't get in. There was no sort of er –

DES: No plan, was there? She came home – 'This is what I'm going to do. Made my mind up now.' She failed the fitness test cause she always carried a bit of teenage weight, you know? She used to say to Doreen –

DOREEN: 'It's not the fitness, it's the fatness, mum.'

DES: I used to – hard as it is to believe – I used to do a lot of running and she got me back out on the roads and we used to go jogging and getting her fit to go into the Army eventually. But I mean she was perfect for them, wasn't she? I would say it was a young person who had recent experience of tremendous upset in their life and then gone through a phase of rebellion and who saw [the Army] as an out.

DOREEN: Believed the adverts – quick fix for problems, I want to do it today, why wait till tomorrow? I think a lot of kids are like that. I don't think she was anything particularly unusual.

JONESY: I was 18 [and] I was walking home from school and I was like, 'Bloody hell, I've got no fags, I've got no money, I'm doing a shit job', and there was no jobs in the Job Centre and the one's that were [were] paying like eighty, ninety pounds a week at the time. I did want more. I'll be honest. I wanted more really. And I was walking past the Army careers, I thought, 'My God, I've never noticed that before.' And I went in and the guy in there was eating Kentucky Fried Chicken. He gave me some of his chips [and he] promised me the world and made me watch a video. Oh, God. That was great. So, I signed up there and then. He said I'd have a ball. And to be fair, he didn't lie to me that much, do you know what I mean? [How long did it take] before I signed my life away? Just under twenty minutes, I think.

DOREEN: I think Cheryl was of the personality that you really had to let her do what she wanted because she would eventually. If she set her mind on something there was no way you would turn her.

DES: Very independent, yeah.

DOREEN: And at the end of the day, she was almost 18, you know, you can't treat them as children, can you? It wasn't what we would have wanted, was it?

DES: No, no, no. There was no plan for that.

DOREEN: We thought, you know, at least they're being looked after, they're not roaming the streets, one o'clock in the morning...she'd be safe...

JONESY: I had to go and sign my Oath of Allegiance. You have to sign in front of an officer which was really impressive, I thought. And nobody believed I was going to go. Even my friends the night I was due to go in, throwing stones at my bedroom window. They were like, 'You don't want to go in there. It's crap!' but I said, 'I'm going.' That was it. Nothing was stopping me. Stood on the train station, my mum and sisters came [to see me off.] I was crapping myself. (*Beat.*) I arrived at Pirbright on a Sunday afternoon in April.

DES: We took [Cheryl] down and had a devil of a job to find the place 'cause of course I'd never thought of that, shows how much I knew. They don't have signs. How do you find it?

DOREEN: That was the worst part, wasn't it? We hadn't realised, had we, till she went through those gates that...

DES: No, [no].

DOREEN: ...we were, you know, that was the parting. She was crying. We were crying. It was awful and coming [home], you know, with an empty car...

DES: It went on forever, didn't it? **[V]**

BLAKE: [On the 14th of May 1995] Cheryl started her Phase 1 training at the Army Training Regiment at Pirbright with a view to joining the Royal Logistics Corps as a supply specialist. **[B3]**

JONESY: 'Get your fucking hands out of your pockets!' **[V]**

BLAKE: Phase 1 training is designed to enhance physical fitness, instil discipline and develop basic military skills. **[B4]**

JONESY: 'Want to join the Army? [You]'re not good enough. [You]'re piles of shit!'

The main purpose of Pirbright is to make you leave. (*Laughs.*) 'Do you want to go home now?' We'd be like starving and pissed wet through and, you know, wondering why you signed that piece of paper and why did I just get won over by a few scabby Kentucky chips? (*Laughs.*) **[V]**

BLAKE: Cheryl's time at Pirbright appears to have been hard work for her, with some concerns as to her fitness and some difficulty in passing her weapons test. [B3]

DOREEN: The first few weeks she was on the phone every day, wasn't she?

DES: [Every day.]

DOREEN: And she was saying – 'Oh, talk to me, Mum, talk to me. No, no, don't go, don't go.' (*Laughs.*) And then obviously – you know, the more they settle in, the less frequent the calls got but – They were there for the first –

DES: Five weeks.

DOREEN: Five weeks without any contact, you know, they were on site.

JONESY: Pirbright was quite hard, that was – physically, 'cause they knock you down and build you up, that's what they used to say 'Knock the civvy out of you[, Jones,] and then rebuild you as a soldier.' Pirbright pushed you to the absolute limit. [But] I think the worst thing the Army can do is become easy. It's gotta live up to its history and its reputation. [V]

BLAKE: [Cheryl James's] Section Commander described her at the first assessment as – 'Another problem recruit…having problems with every area of training.' [B3]

DOREEN: We bought her a mobile. She came home and what was the bill? It was horrendous.

DES: In a matter of weeks she'd clocked up about eighty-nine pound, I think it was…which was a lot of money at the time.

DOREEN: And to be fair, she wrote a lot, didn't she?

DES: Yeah, and we did.

DOREEN: There were always letters flying backwards and forwards. [Excuse me.] [V]

Exit DOREEN.

BLAKE: Her Platoon Commander made the following assessment: 'She has a sense of humour and an agreeable manner which has meant that people are willing to help her.' **[B3]**

JONESY: And the laughs we used to have, oh my God, we used to have some screams in there, you know, like – 'cause you weren't allowed in the NAAFI, you weren't allowed booze or anything like that so what would be the next best thing? Coke, crisps and chocolate. Who was going to leg it? Bear in mind, they had guards and stuff. It always used to be this [one] girl 'cause she was super fit and she could run like the wind. She hated it because there was like eighteen people in our room. [And she's like –] 'How am I going to get back with eighteen cans of Coke?' That was good team building.

DES: There was no issue with Pirbright –none whatsoever. I know when she came [home on leave], I mean she looked fabulous. She'd lost all the weight, all the sort of puppy fat, you know, she was fit, you know, really fit and strong. She looked wonderful. She'd really blossomed.

Gunshots. Enter SWANN, carrying a replica SA-80 rifle, along with ammunition, more slides, etc. He begins to set up a demonstration during the following.

JONESY: We were actually on a run. We were coming through the woods. We heard shots. There was quite a few. The NCO ran to the gate to find out what was going on. He was only twenty seconds and he came back and he was like – 'Come on, we need to get back.'

DES: Cheryl told us. We didn't know any detail and neither did she. **[V]**

Enter CATHCART.

CATHCART: Sean Benton, 20, died from five gunshot wounds to the chest in the early hours of 9th June 1995. [He] was about to be discharged from the Army. [J1]

BLAKE: [The Coroner] recorded a verdict that Sean took his own life. This review is satisfied that: Sean died by his own hand as a result of a deliberate act. The original investigation did not seek to cover up evidence. Sean did not die because he was bullied. Clearly, if there is scientific evidence to exclude the possibility of self-administered injuries, then there must be something wrong with the otherwise clear and consistent witness testimony to the contrary. [B4]

CATHCART: Because police never carried out a proper forensic examination, the account of events can now never be scientifically confirmed. [J1]

SWANN: No forensic tests. The attitude was, 'They're dead. They're a soldier. They've topped theirself.' (*Beat.*) [The SA80] fires between 650 and 700 rounds a minute on automatic. So, consequently it fires approximately thirteen rounds a second. Five shots [have] gone through [Sean Benton's] body. One of them that's over the heart. A death shot to the heart but the other shots were fired first. And they're all distance shots. What it boiled down to was that you could not reproduce that pattern on [Sean] Benton unless you were fourteen feet away. That means Benton would have needed arms fourteen feet long to shoot himself. So, he didn't self-inflict that – but we've got witnesses who said that he did. [V]

Exit SWANN.

CATHCART: There is no doubt that Sean Benton was utterly miserable when he died. Why was he so miserable and how did he die? [J1]

Exit CATHCART.

DES: We didn't react to it. I never remember us having any concerns about it at all. A young boy has shot himself. 'Oh, OK.' Our own daughter was there and we didn't react to it.

Enter DOREEN with video remote control.

DOREEN: [Excuse me], I just wanted to say to Des, would that video of Cheryl be any help?

DES: Yeah, I was going to put it on after.

DOREEN: Oh, right. To see the personality that you're [talking] about. I mean, it's when she was quite a bit younger but – Have you – do you want me to sort it out?

DES: Yeah, well, I know where it is. It's above the desk [with the one of her passing out parade...]

Exit DOREEN.

JONESY: Passing out. That was a good day. Aw, proudest day, that was. You know, that was worth it. Hardest thing to come through and then you're standing on that parade square and we had the Welsh band playing as well. That was mega. Fantastic. Best day. Nothing's ever come close. All your mates around you and now you're looking forwards to your next step and our next step was Deepcut.

DES: It was after the initial training that it all went wrong. [At] Deepcut.

JONESY: We always used to call it Blackdown, I mean, it is in Deepcut, you know, [but] it's known as Blackdown Barracks. It's only since it's been in the media that it's Deepcut. Like it's a deep cut on the people that've died there, I don't know...

DES: She went to Deepcut for a very short time then she went up to Leconfield to do her driver training. Then she came back to Deepcut to wait her posting. She was in Deepcut twice. [V]

CATHCART: Deepcut [was] the very bottom of the pile, it was just a dump, 1,000 trainees passed through Deepcut per year – just out of school, away from home for the first time – they were dumped in Deepcut with not enough to do and no clear idea where they were going. [It] was under-staffed and under-funded. [J1]

JONESY: It's just such a weird camp to understand really 'cause you never really knew who was your NCO or not – you just saw pips, you were like (*Salutes.*) you know, 'Yes, Sergeant' and they could have been, you know, not even Blackdown staff. I just remember this feeling of like you didn't know who was going to be round the corner, that feeling of constantly watching your back. It was just so disorganised. (*Beat.*) I'm sure, that Cheryl was at that camp when we got there but we never really spoke at first, you know. I recognised her accent. That's what made me speak to her. I was like 'Where are you from?' She was like – 'Llangollen.' I was like 'I'm from Rhyl.' She's like – 'No way? Been through it loads of times.' So, that's what got us talking. [V]

BLAKE: There is very little reason to believe any events of significance occurred during Cheryl's first five weeks at Deepcut. She passed a specialist supply training course at the School of Logistics. She would have been available for guard duties when not on trade training. [B3]

CATHCART: Deepcut was out of control with vulnerable young trainees exposed to risks their parents could not have imagined – bullying, sex, drink, and the flouting of rules – notably concerning firearms. [J1] An appalling mess. [V] Former recruits claimed the barracks was run by sadistic NCOs. [J1]

BLAKE: Sergeant B is a complex character. [He] was highly praised by his superior officers for his compassionate concern for young trainees [and] has an unblemished disciplinary record. However by far the most consistent characteristic of Sergeant B is his use of an imaginary 'twin brother' when disciplining trainees. **[B4]**

JONESY: He used it as a management tool which – (*Sighs.*) – I don't know, could that explain itself, I don't know, am I seeping back into Army mentality by accepting it? Now, it would not be tolerated anywhere, I know that now. 'Do you want me to bring my brother out?' 'No, Sergeant.' 'Well, it's too late because he's on his way.' And the next thing he'd just turn into this, like, screaming lunatic. **[V]**

BLAKE: The use of his 'twin brother' clearly endeared [him] to some of the trainees, who saw him as an inspiration, one even citing him as one of the reasons for staying on in the Army. **[B4]**

JONESY: But I wasn't bullied, if that makes sense. It's just constant foreboding and dread, just continuously. **[V]**

BLAKE: Cheryl may have expressed some unhappiness about Army discipline and guard duties, but her parents detected no unhappiness or complaints from [her] at this time. **[B3]**

Enter DOREEN.

DES: One minor doubt when she came home on leave and told us that she had to take beer back.

DOREEN: We didn't take it particularly seriously, did we?

DES: We just thought it was strange and that was the end of it.

DOREEN: She was – she was 17 then because I had to buy it and I thought well, you know, she's nearly 18. We take a can of lager back for the / for the sergeant.

DES: Yeah, for the sergeant, so what like? Maybe there wasn't anything in it, I don't know. It's only all the stuff that's come up since, maybe there wasn't anything in it and we certainly didn't think there was so…

DOREEN: It's just something that happened. **[V]**

BLAKE: [Cheryl] was at the Army School of Mechanical Transport, Leconfield from 31st August until 16th November 1995, [which] seems to have been a happy period for trainees, and Cheryl in particular. Cheryl enjoyed the social side of life. **[B3]**

JONESY: We had such an amazing time there. It highlighted it when we went to Leconfield 'cause we mixed with a whole lot of people and they were from different regiments 'cause we were Logistics, they were in the Engineers and they couldn't believe [it]. They'd be like – 'You're still getting room inspections? They're still beasting you? I can't believe it. Civilians do guard duties in our place and they get paid for it.' We were like (*Laughs.*) 'What?' Everyone was running back 'We want to transfer to the Royal Engineers' they were like 'No chance'.

DES: One of the last times we spent together, she came home on leave and we went walking up over the mountain. We got right to the top and she'd sat in some heather or something and we sat talking. You know, me about self-discipline. I wrote quite a few letters to her while she was in the Army and that was always the theme. She used to take the mick out of me 'cause I was always preaching. And we'd been talking there for a while and I got up and went to walk away and she shouted to me – 'Dad! Don't go just yet. Let's just sit down for a while.' She'd got to the point of young womanhood, you know? I felt we were nearly there. You were starting to have good conversations and views on things and opinions and I mean, she had a good future, you know? **[V]**

BLAKE: The second period that Cheryl spent at Deepcut [followed her return from Leconfield] until her death on 27th November 1995. Although all those who came into contact with Cheryl describe her as a happy, bubbly and fun-loving person, many of her friends note that there was a more fragile, vulnerable side to her personality. **[B3]**

JONESY: I remember [Cheryl] having – this girl, bloody hell, something happened – 'cause you used to get so tired and exhausted. So, you get snappy, don't you? I'm sure it was over cigarettes or something – anyway, they ended up scrapping on the floor and they were absolutely leathering one another. (*Laughs.*) Rolling round, punching, no hair pulling, they were both knocking ten colours out of one another. But the next day they were alright, you know, it was the heat of the moment, it wasn't an underlying thing. So, that kind of stood her in good stead, I think, with others. 'Cause they knew if you pushed her a little bit far, she was going to go, like. She held her own really. **[V]**

CATHCART: Sexual activity was rampant. One official report found that women trainees 'virtually without exception were having regular sexual intercourse in barracks', in breach of rules. When Deepcut's grounds were raked in preparation for an open day, 800 used condoms were collected. **[J1]**

BLAKE: Two relationships with young men feature in the events surrounding [Cheryl's] death. The first is with Private A whom she met whilst they were both training at Leconfield and whose camp was at Blackwater, Camberley which was close enough to Deepcut to enable regular visits. **[B3]**

DES: I think it's been overplayed. You know, we're talking of 17, 18 year old kids, locked up in a camp, out every night, in the pub, having a good time and she's got two boys on the go, so what?

DOREEN: Well, you know, it's like everything else, if you want there to be a reason then you can always find one, can't you? **[V]**

BLAKE: The second relationship was with Private B [and] it is over [this final] weekend that this relationship develops. On Friday 24th November 1995, Cheryl had phoned home to say that she could not come back that weekend because of guard duty. **[B3]**

DOREEN: It was about two o'clock in the afternoon, I think. I used to do a flower arranging class and I'd been out for lunch with the girls, and she phoned, I said 'Oh, you're lucky, you've just caught me, I've only just got here' – and then she was on about Christmas – '[I] haven't done any Christmas shopping yet,' she said, 'and I'm broke.' Well I said, 'join the club but (*Laughs.*) but when you come home we'll go window shopping if nothing else' and that was the conversation. That was the last time I spoke to her.

Exit DOREEN.

JONESY: I wasn't actually on camp. We had a long weekend and I don't know why. (*Beat.*) She was sitting [talking with her friend] on the floor and I said 'Hiya, you alright?' 'Yeah, you alright? You off home?' she said to me. I said 'Yeah. [You?]', she went 'Nuh. [Guard duty.]' I didn't know her that well but I knew her well enough to know that if she wanted to come home, she'd have been in the back of the car and sod 'em. I know she would. [So] I took me bag and I said 'Oh, well, I'll see you when I get back.' [V]

Exit JONESY.

BLAKE: Private B and Cheryl went shopping in Camberley on the Saturday morning [of the 25th November]. They started a sexual relationship back at Deepcut Barracks that evening. [Cheryl's other boyfriend], Private A, entered the room where they were in bed together. Cheryl then spoke to Private A alone. On Sunday 26th November, there was a party in an empty accommodation block. Cheryl spent some time with each of the young men. She was in the male block with Private B until about 02.00hrs on the morning of Monday 27th November, at which time she left to prepare her kit for guard duty. [B3]

CATHCART: When she paraded for guard duty at 6.30am a friend saw her – [J1] 'smile and giggle in her normal way'. [The friend said –] 'Cheryl spoke to me and asked me not to mention that she was sleeping with both Private A and Private B. I told her straight that I thought other people knew about her already anyway and that she should make up her mind, choose one of them and let the other one go gently. [She] was her usual self.' [B3] [So,] the only apparent cloud on her horizon was the need to choose between two boyfriends. [J1]

BLAKE: [The] Lance Corporal [who] paraded the guard did not notice anything wrong with Cheryl's mood. [He said] she did not appear hungover or overly tired. He said he did not smell alcohol on her breath, and would not have assigned her a weapon and ammunition if he had suspected she was not fit to carry out her duties. [B3]

CATHCART: Though Army rules dictated that a woman must never do guard duty alone, Cheryl was dropped on her own, with a rifle, at the Royal Way Gate at about 7am. [J1]

BLAKE: Private B's statement to the Royal Military Police in 1995. He said that he went to meet Cheryl at 07.30hrs at the gate – 'She was happy and laughing...she jokingly said she was going to sit in the woods and let the traffic enter the camp. A Major rode his bicycle through the Royal Way Gate at about 08.15hrs. The gate was then manned by a female guard and he noticed a young man nearby whom he spoke to. The young man knew he should not be there and was told to leave which he said he would. The Major noticed nothing else of significance. [B3]

CATHCART: A staff sergeant, a regimental sergeant major and a captain, were all let in at the gate by Cheryl, one ticking her off for not addressing him as 'Sir'. [J1]

BLAKE: Within the next ten minutes it was to be reported that Cheryl had left the guard post. [B3]

CATHCART: A captain entering the camp noticed that the barrier was up and unmanned. He continued to his office and then reported it. [J1]

BLAKE: A Lance Corporal then drove to the scene to investigate. [He] arrived at the gate and found no sign of Cheryl. Thinking that she may have gone to the toilet, he took over the guard duty. He then became aware of a combat jacket by a tree. He flagged down another Lance Corporal to assist him and together they found Cheryl's body. Her head was pointing down the slope towards the road, with a large wound to the front of her head and an SA80 lying by her side. She was found to be dead. **[B3]**

Enter DOREEN.

DOREEN: I was doing some flower arrangements and the doorbell rang and there was an Army officer and a policeman and I don't know what it was, you just – you think – nothing had registered – anyway, I said come in. 'Mrs James?' What's the problem? 'I'm afraid we can't tell you,' he said. 'Where's your husband?' I said he's in work. What is it? Is it Cheryl? 'I'm sorry, we can't say anything. We have to inform your husband.' It's Cheryl, isn't it? Something's happened to Cheryl…

DES: My closest friend in the company at that time was the personnel manager and I was talking to him in his office. And he was standing by the window and he said 'Oh God, this is trouble,' he said. So, I went over to the window and we both watched this Army officer walking across the car park and coming into reception. (*Beat.*) No association. Nothing. That's how – confident I was… So, I sat there while he went downstairs, maybe I made a phone call or something…and then he came back and he said – 'cause he was experienced – he had a way, you know – and he'd sort of say 'Well, come on then.' And so I followed him down the stairs and we got to the bottom of the stairs and there was an office there then which is not there now, thank God. And the door was open and as we got to the bottom of the stairs instead of turning left into reception he carried on going and sort of almost pushed me in and closed the door. And this bloke was inside… Phew… And that was…bloody hell. He didn't have to tell me, I knew then, didn't I?

DOREEN: This was about half past four in the afternoon now by the time Des comes home and I can remember the Policeman and I were watching Des coming up the drive – [well,] you're in total shock, aren't you? You think it can't be happening, your body's there but you're looking down on things. The policeman said to me – 'You'd better go to him.' And I was standing by the door just watching Des coming up the drive... [V]

CATHCART: Cheryl James was just 18 and a soldier for less than six months when she was found dead. One might have expected this to ring alarm bells with those who knew of Sean Benton's death only 19 weeks earlier, but no – it was immediately assumed she had taken her own life. [J1]

BLAKE: It is clear that, by the standards of investigation into suspicious death, the initial investigation was perfunctory and the opportunity to test key exhibits has been lost. All of this makes it impossible today to demonstrate, beyond doubt, precisely how Cheryl died. [B3]

DOREEN: When someone says [your child has] taken their own life, you are in limbo then totally because you want to know / why.

DES: Everything.

DOREEN: If it's a road accident or any other accident or an illness, there is a reason. But when a fit, healthy, vibrant 18 year old – suddenly you're told that she's taken her own life you – you just – well, Cheryl would not be the type, she was never that sort of person. I know she wouldn't do that. Nobody from Deepcut had come to give us [any] information. We didn't think at the time that it was a shambles. You're not capable of taking it in, you know. I knew Cheryl too well for her to do that. I know people say 'Oh, you don't know people, you don't know' – but I do, I am convinced. The problem is with a suicide –all of a sudden now you have the feeling that it's your fault. I signed the form for her to go into the Army – I'm thinking 'Well, it's all down to us now, isn't it?'

DES: At the time I can remember thinking 'If only, you know, by some miracle I could have just been there that morning.' You know? 'Tell me why you're doing this – if you did – but tell me – just tell me – 'cause I can sort it out', you know?

DOREEN: We'd have gone through hell and high water. That's the other thing, you know, it's so…frustrating, you know, when the likes of Mr Blake and all these people try and tell you what your daughter is like. They did not know her. They have no inkling of her personality and then they give you all this – I mean they said 'Oh, it's all going to come out in the open, she slept with so and so, she's doing this, she's doing that' – well, I don't care if she slept with the whole camp. She did not deserve to die. They think that's some sort of reason. It isn't.

Enter SWANN, again carrying more equipment – photos, laptop, etc.

SWANN: There's certain things connected with [it] that makes it more than suggestible – we're satisfied that she was shot by someone else. Gunshot residue tells you lots of things and where it is on the hands [tells you] whether you were actually holding it and gripping it or whether you were trying to push it away from you and [from the photographs] it shows that she's trying to push the muzzle away from her. **[V]**

BLAKE: From an examination commissioned by Surrey Police self-infliction is a possible and plausible cause of death in this case. A contrary opinion would be completely inconsistent with [this] impressive and persuasive analysis. **[B3]**

CATHCART: Her body was found near some trees lying at 90 degrees to an incline, meaning she would have to have stood or sat at an awkward angle as she shot herself: a position against the tree or with her back to the slope would have been more likely. **[J1]**

SWANN: If she was shooting herself on a slope sitting down, you would have to face away from the slope, if it's steep, which it was – if you attempt to sit sideways on the slope, you roll down the hill. If you attempt to sit facing with your feet up the slope and you've got you're feet at that angle you can't do it. So, you've got to sit the right way round. The positioning of her body and the gunshot residue and everything else doesn't support self-infliction. The forensics support her being shot by somebody else but there was no investigation. Which causes you concern. It does me anyway. [V]

Exit SWANN.

BLAKE: The nature of the injury to the skin was typical of a shot at very close range. The conclusion is that the totality of forensic evidence now available is totally consistent with self-harm, while noting that it is not possible to definitively exclude a third party hypothesis. As there was no sign of a struggle, a third party hypothesis must focus on the proposition that someone known to Cheryl persuaded her to go to the scene of death and hand over the weapon or directed her to use the weapon on herself. No one had any identifiable reason to do this. Cheryl was a popular and much-loved young woman. [B3]

CATHCART: [Private B] gave different accounts of his dealings with her that morning. First he said that after he left Cheryl he saw a mutual friend who was on his way to the gate to apologise to her for something that happened the night before, and that this friend later came back saying he could not find her. The friend, however, flatly denied that the conversation took place, or that he ever went near the gate that morning. Later [Private B] admitted his conversation with Cheryl at the gate was an argument. The earliest independent witness of [Private B]'s presence back at barracks puts him there at about 9am – some 40 minutes after the death. [J1]

BLAKE: This fresh material may lead to Private B being treated with some caution as a reliable historian of the precise details of the sequence of events with Cheryl and the emotional bonds between them. However, they do nothing to suggest a fresh hypothesis as to the cause of her death. [B3]

Exit BLAKE.

JONESY: It was horrendous, that camp when I walked back in there. They were hysterical. A few of them refused to put the uniform on ever again. Her death just absolutely shook the foundations, I think, of everybody. It was straight away – she'd killed herself – no argument about it, no discussion about it. They cleared Cheryl's room. That was quite – frightening, really. I remember walking past her room, they'd left the door open for some reason and – this just empty room and I looked in and they must have opened the window and the net curtain just blew up. (*Beat.*) Wednesday morning we were on a plane and we were out of there. There's so many people that haven't seen each other since the day that she died, since that week. Dunno whether it was done intentionally, I can't say…

CATHCART: It's called 'starbursting'. It's absolutely standard behaviour. When anything goes wrong, everybody gets scattered…

Exit CATHCART.

DES: The following day, I remember I went out and I didn't want to meet anybody but I wanted to get the newspapers, I wanted to see what was being said. I was so desperate to find out what was going on. (*Chuckles.*) So I walked – all in the dark – to the paper shop in [a village] about two mile away. I was there for six o'clock – and bought all the papers that I could find. (*Beat.*) And I wanted him to ask me, I can remember that – I wanted him to ask me. 'Oh, it was your daughter?' But of course, nobody knows, do they? And the perverse thing is I went there because I didn't want him to know me. If you can work that out.

JONESY: I got to Germany on the Wednesday, to my new working unit and they were having a party and I was the only woman there. And this guy said – 'Are you having a beer? I said, 'Yeah, I'm having a beer' so he goes and gets this bottle and I take a drink of it and it's cooled pee. I thought about it very quickly 'cause I thought it's going to make or break me in this unit – I mean, bearing in mind what had just happened and stuff – so I laughed. Would I have laughed if it had happened to someone else? Yes, probably. Happened to me. Heigh-ho. Life, you know? That was it then, you know, kind of fitted in quite well. I can't remember how long I was there but we had a tour of Bosnia coming up and I did really well on that – in fact, I got my first promotion while I was out in Bosnia.

Exit JONESY. Enter DOREEN.

DOREEN: It was horrific. We've had nothing to do with guns or anything like that and I said to [the undertaker], you know, please, if it's so bad, tell us, you know, we want to be prepared. (*Beat.*) We were just lucky we had a very big square hall so it wasn't difficult to do and I know it's an old fashioned thing [but] she had to be home, she had to, you know –

DES: We just wanted to bring her home. So, she came home on the Sunday night and they put the coffin on like two trestles in the hall by the front door.

DOREEN: Horrendous as it might sound, you know, she was home. That did give us some sort of comfort, didn't it?

DES: Oh, yeah, absolutely. It was very comforting that she spent the night there and then the funeral the following day. (*Beat.*) It was in the local church in the village [and] the one thing I can remember is the fact that the undertaker did an old-fashioned funeral. He walked in front of the cars which was quite dramatic and so the traffic stopped and they went right down the middle of the road and he led the thing, you know, it was amazing. And then we – got to the – to the church and erm – /

57

DOREEN: There were so many people they were all outspilling, you know, they were in the garden –

DES: Lining, lining the road, weren't they? Incredible. I remember writing something for the – writing a sort of epitaph.

DOREEN: A eulogy, didn't you?

DES: A eulogy rather and accepting that I couldn't read it myself but I should have done really when I think back 'cause no one else can do it, you know, he – the vicar did it but phew with as much passion as a wet fish. I mean he didn't have a clue, just didn't have a clue, he just – it was just awful – in the midst of all that grief I can remember thinking.

DOREEN: But if people don't know that person they can't –

DES: No, no. But he just didn't do it, did he? He didn't read it I mean it just – anyway, who cares? It doesn't matter, does it?

DOREEN: It was – these youngsters carrying the coffin, it was –

DES: They had some soldiers carrying the coffin up to the grave and they all put their hands over each other's shoulders, you know? Which was quite emotional...

DOREEN: And it was a big thing to expect them to do as well 'cause they were only youngsters, you know, the same age as Cheryl.

DES: They were kids themselves.

DOREEN: And it's probably the first time any of those had ever done it but they did it you know – I can't fault the Army for that day, you know, it was – their behaviour was excellent. (*Beat.*) [She had a Union Jack on her coffin]. And the ber- and her beret and belt and everything – we've still got those...we got them back... [V]

Beat. DOREEN becomes emotional and DES takes up the story.

DES: The inquest into Cheryl's death was held on 21st December 1995. [B3] Four days before Christmas, three weeks after the death, so, you know – world record [time] which again you're in such grief you don't question. The normality is that an inquest is about three, four months after a death so that you have a respectful gap and a suitable investigation.

DOREEN: They'd moved the time apparently to avoid press coverage but they hadn't involved us. It was underway when we arrived.

DES: So, there wasn't a lot of respect going round, you know?

DOREEN: We had to find our own way down there – snowing like mad.

DES: Snowstorm. We left at four in the morning, snowing like crazy, hadn't got a clue whether we'd get there even. It lasted less than an hour. [They'd] had an investigation and it was completed. They'd decided on suicide. [V] (*Reads from a document.*) At the end of the inquest, [the Coroner returned an Open Verdict and concluded -] 'There are missing gaps and I am unable to explain, just as I believe her father is unable to come to terms with, how it is that a girl who one moment seems to be bubbly and outgoing, should the next moment have been found dead with a bullet in her.' [B3] Michael Burgess is the coroner for all the deaths, he did the inquest on [Sean] Benton, he did the inquest on Cheryl, on Geoff Gray and ultimately on James Collinson. He's the Royal Coroner. For me, even today, it's still a mystery that a Coroner can hold an inquest, the second inquest within five months, on the same site, deaths of a similar sort of magnitude and violence and not take some action, you know? Why did he not challenge the investigators that they didn't have any conclusive evidence to support suicide? [Anyway] then we came home and then it was Christmas and I mean, the strangest…how can you imagine Christmas? So, erm – then we go into the New Year and – sorry, it's just for a second.

DES becomes emotional and DOREEN takes up the story.

DOREEN: [There were lots of questions we wanted answered and so you'd started phoning...]

DES: I was phoning first of all. 'Yeah, who's this? OK, this is the RSM Office, yeah, OK hang on we'll put you through.' And then you'd sit there for twenty minutes, nothing happens, so you put it down, ring again, engaged, then you'd ring again, engaged, then you'd ring again, then you get through – 'Yeah, who's that? Yeah, hang on a minute, put you through.'

DOREEN: Just run you ragged, they can run you ragged.

DES: And so you start writing – The first one to the MoD, I wrote on February 26th and I had a reply on April the 30th. That's what you're up against.

DOREEN: They were putting you through to a room. Didn't even have a name.

DES: I was writing to a room. It was just...bizarre. (*Beat.*) I wasn't good, you know. I was having severe depression. I wouldn't talk to anybody. I was down on the floor, you know? I'd drive to work every morning just totally upset and get into the car park, get out and put my face on and go in and then I'd go through the motions of doing my job and go home and then – same – go through the same thing all the time – drinking too much. Didn't care about anything. It's just abject despair, you know? Everything was an effort apart from [writing letters]. That wasn't an effort. I could do that. My wife said, you know, she actually read it in the way I was talking and she said to me – 'I know you've got a death wish, haven't you?'

DOREEN: Is this the way it's going to be? Is this what you're going to do? It's taking your life over, you're not getting anywhere, you've got to move on. You're being obsessive. I mean, to wait ten weeks for a reply – you write three letters, that's a year of your life gone, isn't it? You can't just carry on like that, you're dealing with an institution that's not going to tell you anything. There's no way you're going to get through that armour, no way. You must put it behind you now.

DES: So we got all the files, all of Cheryl's belongings, all of the stuff that was her, put them in boxes, sealed them all up, put them in the attic...

DOREEN: And started to live. [V]

Exit DES and DOREEN.

Beat. Enter CATHCART and SWANN, both have changed clothes and look older.

CATHCART: [Five years later,] in the spring of 2002, researchers from the BBC television programme Frontline Scotland stumbled across what would become a very big story. [J2]

SWANN: Out of the blue, I got contacted by Frontline Scotland who said the parents of the Deepcut Four wanted to know if I would investigate it for them. I said it would cost an awful lot of money because it's probably about six weeks' work. They couldn't afford it. So we decided to do it for a small consideration...which was a pound for each family. We thought that the families and the Army and the MoD, anyone who was involved would want to know the truth. That was the biggest mistake we ever made. [V]

CATHCART: [Frontline Scotland] were looking into the mysterious death of James Collinson and they had already established that a strikingly similar death had occurred at the same barracks just six months earlier. Geoff Gray was only 17 when he was found with two gunshot wounds to the forehead. [J2] Geoff was by all accounts a model trainee, popular, enthusiastic, close to his family. Despite the two bullet wounds, each of which was sufficient to kill, once again there was an immediate assumption of suicide. [J1]

SWANN: When we go to reconstruct the [Geoff] Gray scenario – to do it yourself you've got to be holding it up to here and you [can] see that even with [the replica which is] one fifth of the weight, it's not easy to hold and you've got no control over the front end. The minute you start to fire, it kicks straight up in the air. Gray had one shot here and one shot there. But you can't do it 'cause they're too close together. After the first shot, you can't hit him with the second shot. We conducted tests which we videoed which prove that their story can't be right. We videoed everything. It can't be done. We brought in [a] Regimental Sergeant Major who's a top Army shot and also their instructors – we got them to try and do it – we had to divert it over the shoulder because, you know, not wishing to, you know – and none of them could do it. That was good enough for us. That nobody at all could do it. [V]

CATHCART: The Coroner returned an open verdict [on the 22nd of March] 2002. [B5] (*Beat.*) [The next day], Private James Collinson, from Perth, was found dead while on night guard duty at Deepcut. A single shot had been fired from under his chin and his brains had been blown out. The detective in charge decided James [Collinson]'s death was insufficiently suspicious to merit a full post mortem. [J1]

SWANN: There are photographs of the scene with blood where it's spread about around his body. Now, if you were to shoot yourself underneath here, blood goes upwards and then it starts to go into minute droplets like a mist. The fine mist came down and it should be pretty evenly dispersed. It took us a week of microscopic examination of the photograph to depict the whole area. There was a gap. On the ground. [It] fitted in when we'd measured it up with somebody kneeling. Right next to his left foot. So, there was somebody there as far as we're concerned. That was the basis of us deciding that he'd not shot himself. [V]

CATHCART: Four young people were dead, leaving four grieving families, and no one could or would say why they had died. [J2]

Exit CATHCART and SWANN.

Enter DES. As he speaks, DOREEN enters mid-speech. Both have changed clothes to more formal wear and both have clearly aged.

DES: My sister called me one night [in 2002] and she said, 'There's somebody trying to find you'... Lo and behold, the following morning a letter arrived [from a BBC producer.] It just sort of said – 'I don't know whether you're aware of this but there have been another two deaths, we're looking to do a programme on it, we really would like to talk to you.' I said – 'Listen, we're not doing it and that's the end of it, you know, forget about it now, we've made the decision.' (*Beat.*) I desperately wanted to do it but Doreen simply didn't and didn't want to be involved. [The producer] then rang me back in work and said 'Do you mind if I speak to your wife?' And of course, I knew that Doreen was the one saying no but I said, 'No, of course I don't mind. It's no problem. Just ring her.' And then it was Doreen convincing me to do it which was strange, you know, but I suppose that was part of my plan. [And so Doreen and I] had one of our [Friday night] conversations... (*Beat.*) Well, listen, if this happens it really means we've got to go in the attic, bring it all down [again], open it all up. Remember now, if we do this there's no going back so don't give me a hard time afterwards. If we're doing it, we're doing it. [V]

DOREEN has climbed the step ladder and dislodged a ceiling tile. She reaches in and pulls out a box of Cheryl's belongings. She and DES continue removing box after box after box and stacking them around the stage throughout the following.

Enter CATHCART.

CATHCART: [On June 10th 2002, the families of all four soldiers called for a public inquiry into their deaths.] Deepcut was suddenly national news. **[J3]**

Enter JONESY, now dressed in civilian clothes. She too looks older.

JONESY: I was eating my breakfast one day when the *Daily Post* came in and it was smack bang in the paper…and I went through this whole thing like 'What am I going to do? Am I going to contact them?' and then it just really came in the media and it – I started having nightmares to be honest about it. I kept dreaming about Cheryl, about you know all us lot back there and it was just coming thick and fast. I phoned Des. So, they came here and we met and had a good long chat and I've been in touch with them ever since. **[V]**

CATHCART: The public outcry and questions in Parliament forced Surrey police to upgrade their investigation into the last death and re-open the others. They soon realised they had badly messed up. To this day no one can say for sure who pulled the trigger on the weapons found at the scenes and, indeed, whether those weapons were the ones used. Surrey police made a guarded apology, and with the heat of public scrutiny upon them, threw themselves into a re-investigation covering all four cases. **[J1]**

Enter SWANN.

SWANN: We spent six weeks at Deepcut investigating what had occurred. I got certain vibes about what was going on. To test the water, I said to one of the senior [police] officers that it would probably be a good idea if these were 'accidental' rather than 'suicides'. And he was over the moon. And he went tromping off across the field and immediately used his mobile to ring up HQ and tell them what a wonderful idea, etc, etc. That was the end of the road, as far as I was concerned, because anybody worth his salt would have said 'Look, forget it. What we want is the truth.' But they didn't. (*Beat.*) Now, I made a decision that our reports would be flannelly. Have no scientific basis

whatsoever. Nothing that you can say forensically is wrong
but I put more emotional stuff, because I knew, in my own
mind, that they were going to attempt to alter things and
I didn't want them to alter it until I was ready to publish.
I always took the view from the very beginning that [in] a
public inquiry, I can prove, beyond a shadow of a doubt,
they were not self-inflicted. But there was no way I was
going to prove [it] to the Police or the Army because they
had no intention of accepting it under any circumstances.
(*Beat.*) We used to do police work, Government work,
Treasury, you name it and after Deepcut absolutely
everything stopped and everybody become obstructive
with licensing and all sorts of things and Home Office –
they tried to – well, I say they tried to, maybe that's the
wrong wording – I believed that they were trying to put
us out of business completely. And experience has shown
us that, by delaying things and doing certain things,
they've had a good try. (*Beat.*) You could say and it may be
valid that I have withheld certain evidence and therefore
whatever happens is down to me. So, maybe I made the
wrong decision.

Exit SWANN.

JONESY: The police phoned me up in work and said 'We're
going to take a statement.' Fine. [Then] he said – 'Is there
any good places to go out on the piss?' So, the interview
proceeded from there really, well, if you can call it an
interview… His first question to me was – 'Why do you
think Cheryl killed herself on that camp?' I said, 'Well, I
don't know if she did kill herself, do I? That's why we're
here, isn't it? This is why we're having an investigation.'
He said 'Do you mind if I have a beer?' and I was like
'You're a grown man, yeah, if you must.' We went through
the whole range of things that I'd seen of her character and
her personality and why I didn't think she'd kill herself.
My main point was the uniform. You could always tell
when someone was losing interest or losing pride 'cause
the uniform would go down the pan. But not Cheryl. She

was like a new pin all the time. That was my argument. He asked me about boyfriend swapping, you know, thinking it was funny like, 'So, tell me, how many times did you lot swap boyfriends and girlfriends on that camp?' I thought they were unprofessional and I thought they did Surrey Police a disservice in the way they presented themselves. I got in touch with Des...

DES: Doreen and I had one of our infamous Friday nights.

DOREEN: It was usually Friday because it was the start of the weekend.

DES: It's a bottle of wine and us two.

DOREEN: Oh yes, it's just a wind down, isn't it?

DES: Yeah.

DOREEN: And all the accumulation of events –

DES: Yeah, yeah, while that stuff was going on, of course, there was nothing else to talk about.

DOREEN: Well, no and we were bombarded continually by the press, weren't we, and it was so difficult to stop it affecting your everyday life, wasn't it? So, a Friday night we virtually sort of made a pow-wow, didn't we?

DES: Oh, absolutely. I said, 'You know, I don't feel very comfortable with this lot, I've got [Surrey Police] telling us it'll be over by Christmas, I've got [Jonesy] telling me they're already telling her it's a suicide but they're supposed to be investigating an unexplained death...' [V]

CATHCART: In September 2003, [Surrey Police] produced four separate reports into the [four] deaths. [J1] [In a press release, they stated that] – 'Despite the scale of the investigation, no evidence has come to light so far to indicate any prospect of a prosecution directly related to these deaths.' [E1] At this point, something remarkable happened. The report[s were] not made public, nor was any substantive summary released. [These] key document[s were] not even shown to the dead soldier's families. [Understandably], the families were not satisfied. Such were their complaints that Surrey called in Devon and Cornwall [Police] to review their work. Devon and Cornwall finally completed its investigation into Surrey's handling of the Deepcut deaths in November 2005. That is mired in secrecy too. But a summary [indicated serious concerns about Surrey's 'mindset' towards re-proving suicide.] This prompted a complaint to the Independent Police Complaints Commission that this was hardly an 'open-minded' re-investigation. [J1] The IPCC 'found no evidence of misconduct [and] has accepted that no disciplinary action should be taken'. [E2]

DES: The IPCC is former police officers looking after current police officers, you know, it's not independent at all. Our trust, our faith in the process – you know, you hear it almost weekly – 'The Independent Police Complaints Commission are investigating'. It's said with such authority on the BBC. Doreen and I just sit laughing when we hear it. It's just a joke, you know. [V]

CATHCART: The Police completed a fifth and final report which was to lay bare many of the Army's policy failures. [J1] [On the day of its publication, it was expected that the government or the MoD would make some kind of statement in response. In actual fact, no statement was made. Coincidentally, that self same day, Bruce George MP, the chairman of the House of Commons Defence Select Committee, made a statement indicating that, now the Police investigation was over, the Committee would be holding an inquiry into Deepcut. The press took it and ran with it. Why would we not? It seemed transparent. There was going to be an inquiry into Deepcut. Three weeks later when Bruce George announced the terms of reference for the Committee's 'inquiry' it made no reference to Deepcut. It was to be an examination of all three armed service's 'duty of care' to their recruits. But the press didn't pick up on this subtlety. As far as we were concerned it was still an inquiry into the deaths at Deepcut. (*Beat.*) Now, it's a very serious matter to make accusations of corruption. So, perhaps this was just a case of misrepresentation, or spin. But whichever way you look at it, it wasn't an inquiry into how or why these four young people had died.] (*Beat.*) [On December the 1st 2004, three of the Deepcut families gave] public evidence to [the] Commons select committee. [J2]

Exit CATHCART. The meeting comes to order – BRUCE GEORGE MP, DES and DOREEN.

GEORGE: [I am Bruce George MP, Chairman of this committee.] Ladies and gentlemen, thank you very much for coming along. Our inquiry could not have been complete without the presence of and listening to people whose children died. It must be rather difficult for you and we all appreciate you coming along. Did you get any basic visits from the Commanding Officers or letters of condolence?

DES: The Commanding Officer at Deepcut at the time of Cheryl's death was Lieutenant Colonel Nigel Josling, I am sure you are aware. It may surprise you to know that we were not even aware of that until 2002, seven years after she died. So the answer to the question, did we hear from him, did he speak to us, did we have any correspondence, did we have an apology, I think the answer is obvious.

GEORGE: So you had no letter at all?

DES: Nothing whatsoever. We did not know who he was and still do not know what he looks like.

DOREEN: We did not know his name until 2002.

DES: Can we assume with any confidence that both the Commanding Officers who were commanding the camps when our children died will come before this Committee? Is that intended?

GEORGE: No, that is not intended, I am sorry, but the fact that we are not going to call these guys and do our own personal inquiry is because of our rather tight rules of practice. It does not mean to say we are indifferent to that, but we cannot investigate that.

DES: With respect, Chairman, and at the risk of labouring the point, I am not convinced that taking evidence, even regarding the duty of care issues, simply from the parents and not taking evidence regarding duty of care issues from the Commanding Officers, is not a very one-sided view. Surely to anyone here it makes sense that you talk to the opposite side, because they will have an opinion of the duty of care in place.

GEORGE: Can I say this: if it was any other group talking to us and criticising us for our methodology, I would throw them out. **[E3]**

End of meeting. Exit GEORGE.

DES: It's just another report. Where is it now? Very often I think, you know, how much longer can you just keep this thing going? How many more let downs can you handle? Because it's never-ending.

DOREEN: I think that the feeling to drive on is still stronger than the feeling to give up. And a lot to do with it is the type of personality Cheryl was as well, 'cause you know, Des, you can always hear her in the back of your head – 'Go on, Mum. Go.' You know, she was a pusher. She was fighter. She would never sit back and let things happen, would she?

DES: No, no. She wouldn't have given up, no.

DOREEN: There was never anything negative about her. She was always optimistic. **[V]**

Enter BLAKE who places himself at a lectern and speaks into a microphone.

BLAKE: 15th December 2004. I have been asked to urgently review the information currently available relating to the deaths of four young soldiers in 1995 and 2001 and to report. I have been offered and expect to receive the full cooperation of the Ministry of Defence, the army and the Surrey Police. I hope the announcement of this review will encourage others who have relevant information to come forward if they have not already done so. Those who wish to do so will be able to speak to myself or those assisting me in this review with confidence. **[B6]**

JONESY: QC Blake had no interest in speaking to me whatsoever. I phoned him up, he spoke in a language that I have never heard before. I came off the phone, I was like – 'I've just been baffled by bullshit, I've not got a clue what this man said.' Obviously very intelligent man. Lost me on the fourth word. Came off the phone, emailed Des. (*Beat.*) 'I'm going to tell you [the] verdict of your report now – suicide basically.' (*Beat.*) Is it me? Because I've got rationality, I expect professionalism and somebody's getting paid a lot of money to do a job, they should damn well do the job. You know what I mean?

DES: I firmly believe we shouldn't have taken part in Blake but, of course, if you didn't the Government would say, 'Well, we did try to have an inquiry and you wouldn't take part in it.' So, they've got you. Checkmate. (*Beat.*) A very good friend of mine said to me – 'You can distrust the Police and you can distrust the MoD, but never distrust the judiciary.' **[V]**

Enter COLONEL NIGEL JOSLING. DES, DOREEN, BLAKE, and JOSLING sit for the meeting. BLAKE sets up a tape recorder and pushes the record button.

BLAKE: Shall we introduce ourselves just for the record? I am Nicholas Blake conducting the review.

JOSLING: Nigel Josling. I was the Commanding Officer of what was then called the Training Regiment and Depot in 1994 and 1995 at Deepcut.

DOREEN: Doreen James, Cheryl James' mother, who died in 1995 at Deepcut.

DES: Des James.

BLAKE: I am very grateful to both you, Mr and Mrs James, you, Colonel Josling for coming along today and I hope our meeting will be helpful to all concerned. Can I ask you to say a few words?

JOSLING: Thank you. Yes. First of all, I welcome today's meeting. I hope to be as candid, as co-operative as I can and I hope it will be helpful to you both as an Army Officer in a professional capacity and as a parent with two children of my own, I have every sympathy for you for the deep upset that Cheryl's untimely death must have caused you. So, anything I can do to help bring clarity I would be happy to do so.

DES: You can clarify first of all why it's taken ten years. Lovely words, ten years too late I am afraid.

JOSLING: Sorry, is the point of your question that we have not met before?

DES: The point of my question is you have not been in contact, never met, never offered any sympathy or said anything remotely similar to that before.

JOSLING: Right. Do you recall the day of the inquest?

DES: Just about, yes.

JOSLING: Do you recall after the inquest you were invited back to the barracks and we had a small afternoon tea, reception for you.

DES: Sorry, we don't recall that. We were just hustled out of the – are you saying we went?

JOSLING: In the back of my mind I have the impression that –

DES: For God's sake, come on.

BLAKE: Let's just get the impression. After the inquest, there was a meeting?

JOSLING: We met briefly. That didn't take place in the barracks?

DES: Are you saying it did?

JOSLING: I am asking.

DES: I am definitely saying it didn't.

JOSLING: In that case I must be confusing it with another occasion. However, I am quite certain that I did, in fact, meet the two of you on the day of the inquest. I don't think we actually spoke, but I can remember meeting the two of you.

DOREEN: We have mentioned before it is the possibility we did come in contact that day but it was a very, very brief encounter. I have no recollection of speaking to you or don't even recognise your face. I have got a very good memory and I am sure I would have remembered.

JOSLING: Did you not receive a letter from me?

DES: No. No correspondence.

JOSLING: I have it in the back of my mind – were you living in the Swansea area at the time?

DES: No.

JOSLING: I am almost certain that I did write to you. It seems to me almost unthinkable that I wouldn't as a matter of courtesy have written to you. Let me say now, how very much I appreciate the hurt it would have caused you if you had not received any communication from me, but I can assure you that was not my intent.

BLAKE: Obviously it is a matter of regret.

BLAKE leans forwards and pushes the forward wind button on the tape recorder. We hear the sound of more speech being spooled through before BLAKE pushes the record button again.

DES: There are many indicators collected by Surrey Police and reported to us that Deepcut as a camp was out of control. Do you accept that?

JOSLING: No, I don't. I don't accept it was out of control. There seems to have been some social and even some sexual activity of a nature specifically that we proscribed took place within the barrack bounds, but the suggestion that the camp was out of control I think is an exaggeration.

DES: Okay. So the fact that you had two deaths unexplained, at least ten recorded suicide attempts on the camp in 19 weeks, what does that suggest, that the camp is totally in control, everyone is happy?

JOSLING: It doesn't suggest that everybody is happy, but it doesn't necessarily suggest that the camp is out of control either.

BLAKE forward winds the tape again.

JOSLING: I can remember at the time being shocked, and I am still shocked, that your daughter Cheryl, who had apparently passed through basic training and her trade training without any difficulty – in fact one might almost have said was a model student – I can remember being stunned that she should have found it necessary to do something as desperate as take her own life.

DES: We don't know that.

JOSLING: We don't know.

DES: You are living the assumption. Pardon me, but you are. It was your investigation, the investigation of your officers that made us spend the rest of our lives not knowing what happened to her. There was an assumption made she had taken her own life. There is absolutely no proof.

JOSLING: With respect, Mr James, the investigation was immediately handed over to the Police.

DES: But you still had what amounted to a shambolic investigation into a death on your watch.

JOSLING: I'm afraid that's not strictly correct. The matter was immediately handed over to the Police. So, my involvement and my unit officers' and NCOs' involvement in the investigation was only as witnesses.

DES: You know, we can play with words forever. It was handed over to Surrey Police. Which senior officer was it handed over to exactly? What was his name because I am really getting awfully tired of people playing with words like this. 'Handed over to Surrey Police' could mean the local Bobby turned up in his minivan and said 'I will leave it to you, lads.' Is that what we are talking about or are we talking about a senior police officer who was told 'You have primacy for this investigation. Please conduct it'?

JOSLING: I don't know the answer to your question. I don't know if Mr Blake does. I am sure it is available, but I don't personally know.

BLAKE: There is no senior Surrey Police officer who took responsibility for signing off this investigation in 1995.

DES: Absolutely. **[B7]**

BLAKE stops the tape recorder and returns to the lectern. Exit JOSLING.

DES: [29th of March 2006. Blake finally published his report and] we were invited to go. He would hand out the publication and we would have time to discuss it with him. Doreen and I went down to London.

DOREEN: We were invited to [this building] in Canary Wharf. Massive building, big, flash, like Paddington station. Moving staircases.

DES: [And I was thinking] – 'What the hell are we doing in Canary Wharf? [Why aren't we in Whitehall?']

DOREEN: The way [Mr Blake] came in that morning –

DES: And he was out as quick as he came in, wasn't he?

DOREEN: He could not look us in the face.

DES: No, and he couldn't get out of there quick enough.

DOREEN: He looked down at his books and it was a different man to who we'd spoken to.

BLAKE: [I won't] be announcing a public inquiry.

DES: (*To BLAKE.*) You realise, you don't have to say that. And if you do, you know, for no reason you're going to send us all backward. You know that you're doing that? (*Beat.*) He couldn't look at me, he couldn't answer it. We then asked – surely it made sense for the families to follow Blake and have the same press conference? And they just refused. [So] he went down and did his press conference and we [watched] on a big screen in the room that he'd left us… **[V]**

BLAKE: I welcome you all to this event marking the publication of my report. I am sorry there is so much to absorb in such a short space of time. In order to review the circumstances surrounding the [four] deaths [at Princess Royal Barracks, Deepcut] and the Army's response to them, it was first necessary to see if any conclusions could be reached on how each trainee died. Sean Benton's death was witnessed by two soldiers. It transpires that before and during his time in the Army he had made attempts at self-harm. **[B1]** In the opinion of this Review, the strong likelihood is that Cheryl James fired the fatal bullet at herself with her own rifle at point-blank range. **[B3]** Bullying and abuse played no role in the events leading to the death of Geoff Gray. Although the reasons for [his] death seem baffling, I conclude he most probably killed himself. The recent inquest into the death of James Collinson also suggests that there was no evidence that [bullying and abuse] contributed to his death. **[B1]** In each case the evidence is entirely consistent with self-inflicted death. There is no evidence to suggest another cause of death, and no reason to believe that any such evidence is likely to emerge in the future. **[B8]** If all the lessons that can be learned from these tragic events have now been exposed to public scrutiny and appropriate responses made, there is a very real, and possibly greater, public interest in moving on from events and devoting resources to the well-being of today's trainees. I conclude my remarks by returning to the families whose loss and grief and whose long struggle demands profound sympathy and respect. My conclusions on a public inquiry undoubtedly do not go as far as they may have hoped and wanted, but they should recognise how much they have achieved to date. By their deaths each of these young people have served to help protect others from harm and abuse. Their deaths will not be forgotten. Their lives have not been in vain. **[B1]**

Exit BLAKE.

DES: And that was the end of him, we've never seen him again.

DOREEN: That was supposed to be the be all and end all.

DES: Remember, we can't speak to anybody, we're contained in a room…it was so well orchestrated… We walked out in the end, [not] as any sort of demonstration. For us to have a press conference we have to go across town in a taxi to get to Westminster… By the time we get to Westminster, a lot of the press didn't bother to come because they'd already had their quote. So clever, I mean it's really clever. **[V]** (*Beat. Flash!*) Yes, er, on the face of it er it was a little bit disappointing. Nicholas Blake took us to the brink there – er… **[J4]** In the entire time, that was the lowest day. **[V]** (*Flash!*) We we just have to wait and see which way the government want to take this now and er… **[J4]** I found it difficult to speak to any of the other families. **[V]** (*Flash!*)

Well, I think, it's really – with respect, the way that you phrased that question is is er… **[J4]** I found it difficult to appear confident on interviews. **[V]** (*Flash!*) One of the er one of the problems that we have now with the media is that er the government has convinced the public that there have been so many inquiries into Deepcut, we don't need any more… **[J4]** I was trying to be upbeat and say 'Well, no it's not over because we're going to do this, this and this.' The trouble is I didn't know what we were going to do… **[V]**

Silence as DES stands, beaten and broken. Enter CATHCART.

CATHCART: The news agenda had moved on and the public had registered that the case was closed. Journalists could do little more than pass on a soundbite, which happened also to be the one the MoD desperately wanted in the public domain. There is a message here for campaigners: if at all possible, do not accept or co-operate with a behind-closed-doors investigation. There is also an important message for reporters and editors. Governments, where they can get away with it, will use this device again. They will spring a mass of information on us in the knowledge that we have no hope of processing it in time to meet that day's deadlines, and they know as we know that the second and third day's coverage rarely makes the front page. Journalism dropped the ball. I believe we were outmanoeuvred, tricked by the MoD into letting the matter drop. It was a simple trick and I'm not sure what we could have done about it, but I think at least we should recognise that it happened. Reporters and the public were outwitted. Knowing what we now know, we should expect people to be held to account. Nobody has been. [Not one individual, organisation or institution has ever been held accountable for the deaths at Deepcut. (*Beat.*) The MoD announced the closure of Deepcut and the sale of its land for residential use in January 2008.] **[J2]**

Exit CATHCART.

JONESY: I know people are going to listen to this and think
'Why didn't they just come home? I wouldn't have put
up with that.' Well it isn't as easy as that. Everyone had
a story to tell of why they joined up, what they wanted
to leave behind and they all had too much fire in their
bellies to go under. The Army isn't the easiest option – I
lost count of how many times I was told it was going to be
hard, tough, worst time of your life, you'll be home in a
week – so we accepted the regime, and yeah, we moaned,
but we accepted it and never challenged it even though
we were scared at times. The very thing you miss most, is
the very thing that keeps you there. Your family. They're
so proud, you're so chuffed that they're so proud – you're
out there doing it, succeeding, being the best! I feel I'm
very lucky to be honest. The Army made me and I'd do
it again – differently, but I'd do it again. Deepcut made
me – but it killed Cheryl. How do I face Des and Doreen
and explain that?

*Exit JONESY. DOREEN begins to speak – to the audience, but really
for DES.*

DOREEN: Your strength comes from knowing you're right.
We didn't have that strength eleven years ago but now,
[we] don't care what they say or what they do, really. We
can't be broken any more than we have been, can we?
You know, it'll just bounce off us. They're treating us
like a strategy, aren't they? It's a war game for the MoD.
We're not people, it's something that they've just got to get
around, isn't it? They will not give up. And neither will
we. The alternative is to stop and walk away and I don't
see that as a choice. We've come too far now, you can't
turn back. We don't want to fight against anybody. All we
want is some semblance of the truth, isn't it? [Nothing else
matters] to Des and I. We've lost Cheryl. Can't hurt us
now.

Slowly, quietly, DES begins to speak.

DES: [We have] some rules of engagement. Don't embellish. Don't exaggerate. Don't get hysterical. Tell the truth. Stick to it. That's when they can't handle you. They can't manipulate you when you do that. (*Beat.*) I can't believe in the basic facts. That four families can lose four kids, four families can unanimously, continually and consistently ask for a public inquiry and the Government will do anything at all – apart from that. Now, if somebody can sit me down and explain that, fine. But I can't understand it. And it could have been done, it could have been done by now, a long time ago, you know? So, of course, that leads you to question: 'Why not? What's being hidden?' You know, there's no fairness out there and if people think there is, well, you know, I just hope nothing happens to them. There's no divine right for justice in this country, unfortunately, and I mean that. I'm not just being melodramatic. I really mean that. And that, for me has been a big surprise, you know, I really did think in the beginning, I thought a public inquiry was a formality. How wrong can you be? (*Beat.*) I never think of myself as a campaigner [but] it was a stark realisation for me many months ago that this started out as righting a wrong for Cheryl but now it's more than that. Now, it is very much about righting a wrong, full stop. The biggest part of me accepts that I'll never really know what happened to [Cheryl]. I try not to put myself in a corner where I defend whether it was [suicide] or whether it wasn't 'cause I do believe that it's irrelevant. I really don't care. To me, either way, it doesn't matter. She's gone. (*Beat.*) I'm not looking for people to be on my side 'cause they think I've been treated badly. I want them to be on my side because they believe me and because they believe, as passionately as I do, that we cannot treat each other this way. (*Beat.*) It stops when it's over.

DOREEN: It stops when it's over...

DES: When it's over... [V]

Exit DES and DOREEN.

Lights down. End of play.

Part 2: The Appendices

Appendix A

Timeline

This chronology is not exhaustive and is drawn from the BBC News website timeline and that published as part of the Deepcut Review.

1995

June 9th   Private Sean Benton dies from five gunshot wounds.

July 6th   Inquest into Sean Benton's death held. HM Coroner Michael Burgess records verdict of suicide.

July 10th   Army Board of Inquiry (BoI) into death of Sean Benton.

November 27th   Private Cheryl James dies from single gunshot wound.

December 21st   Inquest into Cheryl James's death held. HM Coroner Michael Burgess records an open verdict.

1996

January 11th   BoI into death of Cheryl James.

2001

September 17th   Private Geoff Gray dies from two gunshot wounds.

2002

March 19th   Inquest into Geoff Gray's death held. HM Coroner Michael Burgess records an open verdict.

March 23rd   Private James Collinson dies from a single gunshot wound.

April 17th   Surrey Police decide to re-investigate the death of Geoff Gray.

May 21st   BBC *Frontline Scotland* programme, 'Deaths at Deepcut', broadcast.

June 10th   The families of all four soldiers call for a public inquiry into their deaths.

June 22nd   Private David Shipley dies in Germany.

     BLAKE: Private David Shipley was found dead in 18 inches of water in a temporary pool at the Gutersloh Garrison, Germany after the Regiment's summer fete. The death was the subject of press reporting drawing a link between his death and the four Deepcut deaths. David was part of the guard force with James Collinson on the night James died [at Deepcut] in March 2002. **[B5]**

July 5th Surrey Police decide to re-investigate the deaths of Sean Benton and Cheryl James.

July 15th Questions asked in Parliament regarding ongoing investigations.

October 1st BBC *Frontline Scotland* programme, 'Deepcut – the Mystery Deepens', broadcast.

November 11th Deepcut & Beyond group formed and call for a public inquiry into all suspicious non-combat deaths in the UK Armed Forces.

Deepcut & Beyond was formed on 11th November 2003 in response of nearly 50 families of soldiers that have died in non-combat situations in coming forward and joining together. They have a common aim in finding out the TRUTH in how and why these deaths were allowed to happen, fighting for JUSTICE to hold to account and prosecute those responsible with a hope that CHANGE will take place to protect other families and prevent future deaths. Over 1750 non-combat deaths have been reported in the last ten years. This figure includes road accidents and genuine natural causes. Other deaths are not as easily explained and are not fully investigated by the MoD, and over 200 of these deaths are firearm-related. **[O1]**

November 29th Minister for the Armed Forces Adam Ingram gives go-ahead for Forensics expert Frank Swann to enter Deepcut barracks.

2003

January 13th Frank Swann enters Deepcut and begins investigations.

February 17th Amnesty International backs calls for a public inquiry.

August 2nd Surrey Police postpone announcing findings after receiving reports from Frank Swann.

September 19th Surrey Police provide HM Coroner Michael Burgess with their reports, brief the families, publicly apologise for not retaining primacy in relation to first three deaths and announce intention to publish fifth report.

The House of Commons Defence Select Committee (HCDSC) announces its intention to conduct an investigation with Terms of Reference to follow.

September 22nd Mr and Mrs James make formal complaint against Surrey Police regarding misleading information on MoD Police involvement.

Devon & Cornwall Police appointed to review Surrey investigations.

October 13th HM Coroner Michael Burgess decides not to hold fresh inquests into first three deaths.

2004

March 4th Surrey Police publish their 'Fifth Report' which highlights Army failures to learn from past mistakes and reports.

March 19th HCDSC publishes its terms of reference – intends to investigate 'Duty of Care' in the Armed Forces.

April 27th Adjournment debate held at Westminster Hall – Defence Secretary Geoff Hoon rules out possibility of a public inquiry.

May 24th Adam Ingram commissions Adult Learning Inspectorate (ALI) to conduct investigation of military training establishments.

July 19th Surrey Police apologise to Mr and Mrs James for misleading them about MoD Police involvement in investigations.

September 7th Army instructor Leslie Skinner is convicted for indecent assaults of male soldiers at Deepcut between 1992 and 1997.

November 30th Adam Ingram announces independent review.

December 1st Three of four families give evidence to HCDSC.

December 2nd Channel 4 *Dispatches* programme, 'Barrack Room Bullies', broadcast.

December 15th Appointment of Nicholas Blake QC to conduct Deepcut Review announced.

2005

March 14th HCDSC Report published – accuses Army of failing in way it handles new recruits and allowing bullying to go unreported. Recommends independent complaints panel but does not call for a public inquiry.

March 21st　ALI report published. Calls for reform of training in all three Armed Forces. Says risks to recruits are too high.

March 22nd　Nicholas Blake appeals for service personnel to come forward and speak to his Deepcut Review.

August　Devon & Cornwall Review reports to Surrey Police.

August 10th　Inquest into death of David Shipley records open verdict.

> BLAKE: The Coroner who conducted the inquest found no evidence of victimisation of David in Germany, although he was not entirely happy with the evidence of how David died. **[B5]**

> PRESS: South Cumbria and Furness coroner Mr Ian Smith said that evidence he had heard from soldiers had all the hallmarks of a concocted story. **[J5]**

> CORONER: The evidence does not further or fully disclose the means by which the death arose. We have our suspicions. We don't really have any fact to go on. **[J6]**

November 4th　Surrey Police publish three-page summary of Devon & Cornwall Review.

2006

March 10th　Inquest into death of James Collinson records open verdict. HM Coroner Michael Burgess says MoD should have nothing to fear from a public inquiry.

March 29th　Nicholas Blake QC publishes the Deepcut Review. He asserts that the first three deaths were 'on the balance of probability' self-inflicted. He does not call for a public inquiry.

June 13th　Adam Ingram responds to the Deepcut Review. Rejects Independent Ombudsman but instead plans to establish an independent commissioner to monitor chain of command.

July 11th　Independent Police Complaints Commission completes inquiry into complaint made by Mr and Mrs Gray regarding Surrey Police 'mindset' and rejects Devon & Cornwall concerns on same issue.

September 15th 'Deepcut: Shots in the Dark' by Heather Mills and
Brian Cathcart published in *Private Eye* magazine.
(Appendix B1)

2007

February 26th 'How the Government outmanoeuvred the media'
by Brian Cathcart published in *The Guardian*, with a
longer version appearing in *British Journalism Review*.
(Appendix B2)

June 11th Des James calls for publication of Devon & Cornwall
Review after leaked minutes suggest Cheryl's death
should have been treated as murder.

2008

January 8th Armed Forces Minister Bob Ainsworth MP
announces that Deepcut barracks will be closed in
2013 and its land sold for residential use.

Appendix B1

Deepcut – Shots in the dark

A Private Eye *special report*
By Heather Mills and Brian Cathcart, 15/9/2006

When Nicholas Blake QC published his report last March into three of the four deaths of young recruits at the Deepcut Army barracks in Surrey, he concluded that all were probably suicides, that the trainees themselves were solely to blame, that they hadn't been 'bullied to death' and that a public inquiry would serve no purpose.

Delighted ministers declared the Deepcut affair was over: there had been no murders; there was no need for a public inquiry; and problems at the barracks had largely been dealt with so there was nothing more to be said. Just as they had hoped, discussion in the media petered out in days and a scandal that had caused public concern for four years seemed to be fading into history.

On closer inspection, however, the 400-page Blake report (with hundreds more pages of appendices) raises many more questions than it answers. Far from being 'the last word' on the matter, the muddled and incomplete report merely demonstrates once more the need for a full public inquiry – something the bereaved families have been demanding for years.

Despite early reservations about the limited and behind-closed-doors character of Blake's review, the families were persuaded to put their trust in the QC, a respected human rights barrister. But now they feel betrayed and let down on the grounds that:

- Blake was a credulous investigator – cherry-picking statements that supported his theories and neglecting those that did not. He interviewed the higher ranking army personnel but ignored those who were at the scenes, and rarely questioned the word of army or police officers who insisted nothing was wrong.
- He made evidence public for the first time that often contradicts accounts of the deaths, yet still declares that 'on the balance of probabilities' there was no mystery.
- Though large amounts of evidence point to a culture of bullying and sexual and psychological abuse at Deepcut, Blake fails to call those responsible to account – and in many cases makes excuses for them.
- Though he had abundant evidence that Sean Benton suffered sustained bullying at the barracks, he rejected this factor in his death.
- Though the initial police investigations into at least three of the four deaths were grossly incompetent, with evidence neglected, lost or destroyed, Blake never criticises the Police.

- Though the evidence points to disastrous failures of management at Deepcut and a *deliberate* army refusal to address key problems, Blake failed to call a single senior officer to account.
- Blake failed to challenge – or even recognise – a long history of cover-up and obfuscation by the army, the Police and the MoD.
- When his report was published he stood up as the MoD choreographed events and spun his findings to ensure that the official line – that the Deepcut affair was over – had maximum prominence. The families had barely an hour to digest the review, take on board its new revelations and ask questions.

Blake certainly failed to get to the source of the stink emanating from Deepcut. And there is a stink. The four deaths at the barracks, whether they were suicides or worse (and that still cannot be ruled out), were extreme symptoms of a dangerous malaise in the British army's training system; a malaise which affected the youngest and rawest recruits in the Armed Forces, which went on for years, was the result of official army policy and which was prolonged by a negligent failure to address glaring problems.

The details, treated almost blandly by Blake, make shocking reading...

THE POLICE INVESTIGATION
Knackered from the start

It was to take seven years and four violent deaths before clues started emerging that something was terribly wrong at Deepcut, the sprawling training barracks near Camberley, Surrey. First, two sets of grieving parents had both lost sons – Geoff Gray and James Collinson, both 17 – within six months; then a television researcher with BBC Scotland made the discovery that two more families – those of Sean Benton, 20, and Cheryl James, 18, had suffered in just the same way a few years earlier.

With four dead – all young, all on guard duty, all killed by gunshots and all rubber-stamped as suicides, Deepcut became national news. Concern mounted as former recruits claimed the barracks was run by sadistic non-commissioned officers (NCOs) and that bullying and sexual harassment were rampant. Frank Swann, an independent ballistics expert, who spent six weeks at the base, started to question whether the recruits could have shot themselves in the manner described.

The ensuing public outcry and questions in Parliament forced Surrey Police to upgrade their investigation into the last death and reopen the others. They soon realised they had badly messed up.

In the first three cases they failed to 'assert primacy' over the military police, while the military police certainly weren't asserting any primacy of their own. In short, no one ran these enquiries; they were presumed suicides and left at that.

The result was lost evidence. The usual forensic essentials of a violent death investigation – securing the scene, a minute search, fingerprinting, swabbing, tracing, expert examination of the body and weapon – were ignored. Records and uniforms were destroyed, witnesses were not interviewed, hypotheses were not tested. To this day no one can say for sure who pulled the trigger on the weapons found at the scenes and, indeed, whether those weapons were the ones used.

Once Surrey Police spotted the scale of their errors, they made a guarded apology. They were sorry, they said, 'for not properly challenging early assumptions that these young soldiers had taken their own lives and for our failure to overturn the custom and practice of the day, which allowed for the investigation to be delegated to the army'.

It looked like a sly attempt to blame the army, and as for the custom and practice, well, no record of it exists. But having made a mess once, and with the heat of public scrutiny upon them, Surrey Police threw themselves into a re-investigation covering all four cases. In September 2003 the force produced four separate reports into the deaths – of Sean Benton and Cheryl James in 1995, of Geoff Gray in 2001 and of James Collinson in 2002. Incredibly, these were not published and were not released to the bereaved families.

The only known fact of substance is one line from a statement by Bob Quick, then Surrey's Deputy Chief Constable: 'No evidence has come to light so far to indicate any prospect of a prosecution directly related to these deaths'.

Degrading acts

Not surprisingly, the families were not satisfied. Such were their complaints that Surrey called in Devon & Cornwall Constabulary to review their work. The following March, Surrey Police completed a fifth and final report which was to lay bare many of the army's policy failures. Of course, as with everything else in the Deepcut affair, much of the detail remains suppressed, but that report did prompt a Commons Defence Select Committee inquiry into the army's general Duty of Care towards young recruits. That was highly critical and brought into the public domain shocking allegations about the base.

Surrey had received allegations from 118 recruits and former recruits of sexual assault, including rape, bullying, harassment and recruits being made to carry out degrading acts such as being forced to strip and parade naked. When in October 2004, Leslie Skinner, an army instructor, was convicted for sexual assaults on male recruits at Deepcut and elsewhere, the demands for a public inquiry were becoming irresistible.

The government's response was to bring in Nicholas Blake, a respected human rights QC, as a halfway measure to 'review' the evidence. At first, some of the families were reluctant to co-operate, but eventually they agreed – at least someone independent of the state would get to look at the evidence.

Blake was nearly a year into his review when Devon & Cornwall finally completed its investigation into Surrey Police's handling of the Deepcut deaths. That is mired in secrecy too, but a summary published in November 2005 made alarming reading. The review team thought that some of what they saw was muddled and wrong-headed. The top brass in Surrey, it seems, interfered so much that it wasn't clear who was really in charge. Worse, there was no auditable decision-making process. When a written set of 'initial strategic aims' was found, Surrey officers denied all knowledge of them – perhaps not surprisingly, because the original read: 'Slowly turn the media focus away from murder, turn spotlight of criticism on to the army and move from how they died to why'. Geoff Gray's family had obtained under the Freedom of Information Act an army email which said of the Surrey Police re-investigation: 'police admitted that the investigation will have the same result – suicide'.

This prompted a complaint to the Independent Police Complaints Commission that this was hardly an 'open minded' re-investigation. The IPCC rejected the complaint.

Screwed up

Blake met with Devon & Cornwall police in November 2005 – two months before he concluded his own review. This gave him little time to re-appraise the evidence gleaned by Surrey – evidence that he relied upon to reach his conclusions. In fact, he ignored Devon & Cornwall's criticisms and declared Surrey's investigations from 2002 onward as 'thorough and exhaustive'.

But as all the reports remain a secret shared between Surrey and Blake, we are asked to take it on trust that the same force that screwed up the investigations once will have got them completely right the second time.

THE SHOOTINGS

1. Sean Benton

Sean Benton, 20, died from five gunshot wounds to the chest – two on one side and three on the other – in the early hours of 9 June 1995. The recruit from Hastings, East Sussex, was about to be discharged from the army. With just five days left on a three-month warning for kicking in a window, Sean had threatened a woman NCO after she told him he would be on guard duty over the coming weekend.

On 8 June Major Robert Gascoigne fined him £150 for the offence and said he would be applying for his discharge. Because Sean had a history of self-harm, Major Gascoigne said that a decision was taken that, in the meantime, his duties should not include carrying a weapon. He was apparently supervised during the evening, but left alone in the bar at about 11.20 that night.

Sean eventually tricked a young guard into handing over her SA80 automatic rifle by saying he was wanted in the guardroom. He then headed off on a lone patrol in the direction of the officer's mess. Soon another guard reported hearing a shot and the news was radioed to the guardroom.

The duty corporal grabbed a weapon and ammunition and with a woman private drove towards the scene. Both initially described how they saw Sean sitting with his back to the perimeter fence. The corporal shouted to him to put the weapon down but they heard a burst of gunfire and saw Sean's body lurch over. The private kicked the weapon away from Sean's body and the pair tried to staunch the bleeding, but by the time an ambulance arrived Sean Benton was dead.

Three notes were found near the body, one to his parents, one to a sergeant and a third to a friend. When police arrived it appeared to be a clear case of suicide and an inquest decided that Sean had shot himself.

However, family members were not so sure, and after learning of Cheryl James's death at Deepcut in November that year, they and their MP began to ask questions. How, if only one shot was fired at close range, could Sean have fired the other four? And if army rules had been followed, could his death have been prevented.

More than ten years later, the Blake report sheds important new light on these events. When the woman private who said she witnessed Sean's death spoke to Surrey Police in 2003, her story was significantly different from what the inquest heard in 1995.

First, both she and the corporal revealed that when they heard that Sean had a rifle, their first thoughts was that he might use it to threaten a particular lieutenant they knew he hated (and whom other recruits hated too). More important, as she and the corporal ran towards Sean, she now said that Sean fired a shot in her direction. She then shouted at the corporal to return fire – to shoot at Sean – and was angry when, she says, he did not.

This casts Sean's death in a new light. If the private was right, her companion had the means – a readied rifle – and a legitimate reason to shoot. This in turn lent significance to another strange fact: the duty corporal's weapon was found to be short of one round (he denied firing it, saying he must have missed one cartridge when loading – though a witness who saw the loading remembered differently).

Because police never carried out a proper forensic examination of the scene, the body or the two weapons, the corporal's account of events can never now be scientifically confirmed. Incredibly, Sean's bloodstained jacket was swiftly laundered.

Blake, however, relied on reports prepared much later for Surrey Police by the German Federal Crime Bureau, the BKA, based on photographs, post-mortem reports and the remaining traces on Sean's jacket. They concluded that the two wounds on his right side were inflicted first, followed by the three on the left. Deposits found around all five bullet holes, moreover, indicated that none was fired from more than 10cm away.

But Frank Swann, an independent ballistics expert who was first to look at the case, said that given the rapid speed at which the SA80 fires when set to automatic – 10 to 13 rounds per second – Sean's wounds would have been closer together if he had fired them himself. Swann believed that only one wound appeared to have been made at close range and the others were fired from at least 14ft. (Swann maintains that Surrey Police called off a meeting between ballistics experts, including him, after he insisted on making his own video of proceedings – so he had a copy as well as the Police. Consequently he says he will now *only* make his findings available to a public inquiry. But this means his evidence remains secret and untested).

According to the BKA, Sean must have shot himself first from a standing position and then from a kneeling one – yet the eyewitnesses described him sitting with his back to the fence. (Only later did one of them 'accept' that 'it could be more likely' that he was kneeling.)

Blake accepts this and also concludes that the woman private was simply mistaken when she said Sean fired in her direction. The 'whoosh' she heard must have been a missed round heading into the open, he decided.

For Sean Benton's family and their legal advisers there are major difficulties here, of which the biggest is that the BKA ballistics reports remain, like so many other Deepcut documents, secret. But in the face of all this complicated and contradictory new evidence, Blake concludes that a new inquest, or indeed a public inquiry, wouldn't change the original suicide verdict.

Even if Blake is right and Sean did commit suicide, Blake himself reveals a catalogue of claims from recruits indicating that Sean was the victim of bullying by both sadistic NCOs and fellow recruits. One admitted being part of a group who, wearing gas masks, attacked Sean in his bed at night. And more than one suggested that Sean was often singled out by both the same corporal who saw Sean shoot himself, and by the sergeant who was in charge that night – a man Blake calls Sergeant B, but who has been identified in the media as Sgt Andrew Gavaghan.

Many witnesses described Gavaghan as a Jekyll and Hyde personality, charming to those he favoured and vile to those he did not. He himself spoke of a fictional 'twin brother' into whom he turned when angry – he called this a 'management tool'. One recruit said: 'I have seen Sgt Gavaghan for an unknown reason punch Sean in the chest and would pick Benton out of the parade and humiliate him in front of us. I can recall one incident when Sgt Gavaghan got Benton out and made him lay down and he was punched in the leg, given a dead leg.'

Several recruits described how they saw Gavaghan or the corporal punch and or kick Sean. 'The corporal was just an out and out bully and an extension of Sgt Gavaghan, in fact his right arm for punishments.'

Blake had evidence from Sean's parents that when he was last home on leave, the previous May, he was unhappy and did not want to go back – although he made no complaint of bullying. Blake also had evidence to show that Sean lost well over three stone in weight in the six months before his death – at post-mortem he was 8st 7lbs.

But what does Blake conclude, in the face of all this evidence? At one point he says there is substantial evidence suggesting Sean was bullied. Later, he declares that it is difficult to reach any conclusion on whether Sean was the victim of bullying. Next he points out that Sean himself did not complain about bullying and says it would be a disservice to Sean's memory 'merely to characterise him as a victim of bullying'.

Finally Blake decides that Sean Benton died as a result of 'his own deliberate act' and that 'bullying by NCOs or otherwise played no part'.

There is no doubt Sean Benton was utterly miserable when he died. Why was he so miserable and how did he die? Blake does not provide adequate answers. What he does do, is prove that only a public inquiry can.

2. Cheryl James

Cheryl James was just 18 and a soldier for less than six months when she was found dead, with a single bullet wound almost between the eyes, on the morning of 27 November 1995.

When she paraded for guard duty at 6.30am a friend saw her 'smile and giggle in her normal way', and the lance corporal who drove her to her post said she 'appeared to be her normal happy self'. She had been out the previous weekend buying Christmas presents for her family and the only apparent cloud on her horizon was the need to choose between two army boyfriends.

Though Army rules dictated that a woman must never do guard duty alone, Cheryl was dropped on her own, with a rifle, at the Royal Way gate at about 7am.

Her boyfriend (of the two, this was the newer) said he went to see her there at 7.30 and was told to leave by a major who passed by at 8.15. He said they kissed goodbye and arranged to meet later.

In the next few minutes a staff sergeant, a regimental sergeant major and a captain, were all let in at the gate by Cheryl, one ticking her off for not addressing him as 'Sir'. But then a captain entering the camp noticed that the barrier was up and unmanned. He continued to his office and then reported it.

A lance corporal drove to the gate to find no sign of Cheryl. Believing she may have gone to the toilet he manned the gate himself for a few minutes before noticing something in the trees nearby. He flagged down another lance corporal and together they found Cheryl's body, her weapon at her side.

One might have expected this to ring alarm bells with those who knew of Sean Benton's death only 19 weeks earlier, but no – it was immediately assumed she had taken her own life and another slapdash investigation ensued.

The Surrey coroner later recorded an open verdict, saying he was 'unable to explain how it is that a girl who one moment seems to be bubbly and outgoing should the next be found with a bullet in her'. Once again time would shed a different light on events.

For when Surrey reopened the case after the fourth death at Deepcut in 2002, Cheryl's boyfriend gave different accounts of his dealings with her that morning.

First he said that after he left Cheryl he saw a mutual friend who was on his way to the gate to apologise to her for something that happened the night before, and that this friend later came back saying he could not find her. The friend, however, flatly denied that the conversation took place, or that he ever went near the gate that morning.

Later the boyfriend admitted his conversation with Cheryl at the gate was an argument. He knew she had seen her old boyfriend the night before and he said Cheryl had made a sexual comment which concerned him. He said Cheryl had told him she was going to sit in the trees and let the cars in.

Blake sees nothing suspicious about the boyfriend changing his story, concluding blandly that he 'should be treated with some caution' as a witness.

Once again all efforts to understand what happened are hampered by the failure to carry out even a basic forensic examination of the scene, the body or the weapon. The BKA, working on the slender information available, decided that although Cheryl's death was consistent with self-harm it was impossible to rule out the involvement of a third party.

But Blake does just that: he rules out third party involvement. He says that the site was too busy and exposed for a premeditated attack (he doesn't even consider a spontaneous one) and since there was no sign of struggle Cheryl could only have been persuaded to go into the trees by someone she knew.

Blake recognises that the boyfriend was the only plausible candidate for luring her away from her post – but says there is no evidence to suggest that he did persuade her or wanted to. Yet the boyfriend had opportunity, means and a possible motive. And although the major ordered him to leave the gate at 8.15, *he did not see him go.* Moreover, the earliest independent witness of the boyfriend's presence back at barracks puts him there at about 9am – some 40 minutes after the death.

Frank Swann, the independent ballistics expert, believes murder a more likely scenario. Her body was found near some trees lying at 90 degrees to an incline, meaning she would have to have stood or sat at an awkward angle as she shot herself; a position against the tree or with her back to the slope would have been more likely. Both the position of her hands and the black deposits pictured on them was consistent with her trying to force the weapon away from her face.

Instead Blake focuses on suicide and speculates that Cheryl's love life was causing her more concern than she outwardly displayed. He cites witnesses who said she had rows over cheating on her old boyfriend.

Blake also makes much of a psychological profile of Cheryl drawn up more than seven years later. But this was built up largely from the state-ments of friends at Deepcut, where she had been for only six months. They included the new boyfriend, who barely knew her. Her family were not asked to contribute.

Central to the profile, and also to Blake's reasoning about Cheryl, was her so-called history of self-harm. This was based on the suggestion that at the age of 15, following the suicide of a cousin, she had taken a drug overdose.

This does not reflect the full facts. According to her father, shortly after the cousin's death Cheryl announced to a friend at school that she had taken some tablets; the friend told a teacher and Cheryl was taken to hospital. There was no treatment and Cheryl said later she had taken five paraceta-mol. Afterwards, in fact, she assured her parents she could never inflict the sort of pain on her family that was caused by her cousin's suicide.

In order to make the case for suicide Blake also relies on evidence which he admits was 'considered too slight to be called before the inquest' – a conversation allegedly overheard by an electrician, in which Cheryl supposedly said that if you can't afford to buy yourself out of the army, then the only way out was to put a gun to your head.

Blake, in his report, mentions what 'fair-minded people' might think. They might think, even on the evidence that they have been allowed to see, that the story of Cheryl's death is a lot more complicated than the simple suicide which Blake accepts.

3. Geoff Gray

Geoff Gray was only 17 when he was found with two gunshot wounds to the forehead, one above each eye, in the early hours of 17 September 2001. He had been on guard at the officer's mess with two other privates when he said he was going to patrol alone. Three to five minutes later his fellow guards heard what they described as a single shot, followed a split second later by a burst of fire. Others too reported hearing shots at about 01.15.

This was a week after 9/11 and the base was on heightened alert. The sergeant in the guardroom ordered his deputy to take two armed guards and head towards the officer's mess. When they got to the gate which Geoff had left, his fellow guards were agitated. One had his weapon loaded, announcing he was 'ready to kill'. He was apparently told to calm down.

The other three then went to search for Geoff. Although it was a small area, they found nothing and called for assistance. More than an hour passed before they spotted Geoff's body – in a spot one of them insisted they had searched. As they approached they heard what they thought was the fence rattling, and one said he thought he saw someone running away on the other side.

Despite the suggestion of an intruder, and despite the two bullet wounds to the head, each of them was sufficient to kill, once again there was an immediate assumption of suicide and the area was not treated as a crime scene. Just how poorly it was searched was revealed when Surrey Police returned to the scene much later, after the fourth Deepcut death, and found a piece of human skull. It was Geoff's.

Geoff was by all accounts a model trainee, popular, enthusiastic, close to his family and on good terms with his old girlfriends. On the night he died he had been in touch with one of them, making arrangements to meet. He was an unlikely suicide case.

Earlier in his guard shift Geoff had been involved in an ugly confrontation with a civilian fire officer at the gate. The civilian was drunk, threatening and abusive to Geoff and his female guard companion, and he had no military ID. An NCO alerted by Geoff on the radio came to the gate and both men escorted the drunk to the officer's mess, where he was living and where his identity was confirmed.

Blake is convinced that the drunk played no part in Geoff's death, but although two army officers said they checked on him in his room in the officer's mess later that night, their evidence is not conclusive and it is not clear whether the man himself was ever interviewed by Surrey Police.

Blake dismisses concerns about what happened to Geoff Gray's weapon after his death, and attempts to reassure by describing in detail how it was passed between police forces and experts and apparently still remains with Surrey Police. What he fails to explain is that the weapon log – which could have proved that the weapon now with Surrey Police was indeed the one allocated to Geoff that night – was removed from the armoury that night and shredded.

Once again the BKA, relying on photographs, witness statements, Geoff's damaged beret and other fragments, concluded that while the involvement of a third party cannot be ruled out, his injuries were consistent with suicide. Once again Frank Swann maintains that the angle and distance between the two wounds – either one of which would have been instantly fatal – makes suicide highly unlikely. He had an unexplained bruise to his right shoulder and the position of his boy with his head some 30cms from the perimeter fence and his feet pointing towards the side of a tree were consistent with being ambushed.

Blake (unlike the inquest which returned an open verdict) concludes that the balance of probabilities indicates that Geoff Gray killed himself. A killer, he argues, would have had to take Geoff's weapon without a struggle and then shoot him at near point-blank range. Unless he had his own weapon and swapped it for Geoff's after firing.

Blake *is* perplexed why a healthy, enthusiastic recruit would kill himself, but again he makes a special effort to find suicidal tendencies. Apparently Geoff was quiet after he spoke to a girlfriend that night and had earlier complained of boredom after two 24-hour guard duties, saying 'I feel like shooting myself'. But the most bizarre leap of logic relates to Geoff's mobile phone. Stored among the phone numbers was this: 'Date died… 1744'.

Geoff died in the early hours of the 17th of the month and this entry was stored at entry number 16 (to Blake, in a Dan Brown moment, the night before) and he seized upon it to suggest that 'if it was inserted by Geoff, it provides further support for a morbid state of mind on the night of 16th September 2001'. It was in fact Geoff's odd way of remembering his bank account pin numbers.

In his keenness to see the death as a suicide Blake even puts forward the proposition, which Geoff's parents find ridiculous, that he was simply curious to know what it is like to shoot oneself with a powerful weapon.

Again a 'fair-minded' person might want an adequate explanation as to why it took so long to find Geoff's body, for the bruising on his body, as to why the Police didn't take more interest, what the drunken fire officer has to say for himself and what the forensic reports actually show.

4. James Collinson

Private James Collinson, from Perth, was 17 years and three months old when he was found dead from a single gunshot wound to the head while on night guard duty at Deepcut on 22 March 2002 – four days after the inquest into the death of Geoff Gray.

Last March, after a three-week inquest, a jury was presented with a choice of possible findings: suicide, accidental death and an open verdict, the last of which was defined as meaning that 'the evidence does not fully disclose the means whereby cause of death arose'. They recorded an open verdict.

Blake's review did not look at this case in detail, leaving it to the inquest: this is why his findings relate only to the first three deaths.

Superficially the evidence in the Collinson case seemed to point to suicide. Another trainee testified that James had borrowed his gun, saying that he wanted to go on patrol so that he could smoke a cigarette (forbidden while on guard duty). Shortly afterwards a shot rang out and a few minutes later James's body was found near the perimeter fence, the rifle at his side.

A single shot had been fired from under his chin and his brains had been blown out. It was the gun at his side that had fired this bullet; one shot was missing from its magazine. Two other young soldiers later testified that James had spoken that same night of his intention to kill himself.

As the inquest jury found, however, it was not as simple as it seemed. For a start, pretty well everything about James's life and conduct in the previous hours and days pointed to a mood of optimism and confidence.

The army itself acknowledged that James was on course for a successful career in one of the most glamorous jobs his corps could offer: as an air despatcher. He was also, according to those who knew him, fun-loving, a joker, popular, full of life and 'army-barmy' – he had dreamed of enlisting since childhood. James Collinson was on nobody's at-risk list, nor was he a victim of bullying. So what about the suggestion that he spoke of suicide?

Private Michael Foody testified that James, while watching television in the guardhouse before going on duty, said: 'If I have a rifle tonight, I'll kill myself.' He said it was said in a light way and no one took it seriously. But although Foody said between six and eight others were in the room, no one else said they heard the remark.

Private Scott Smith testified that later that evening, when travelling by minibus to the guard gate, James made a very similar comment. Again, though others were present no one else heard this, and, like Foody, Smith did not report it until after James's death.

Everyone else who spoke to James that night reported him to be in his usual good form. As he boarded the minibus he spotted his girlfriend, a fellow soldier, and made an arrangement to see her later, saying excitedly that he had something to tell her.

By this time Deepcut had stopped issuing guns to soldiers under 17 years and 6 months, so James went on guard duty armed only with a torch, and was accompanied by two armed older trainees, John Donnelly and Stacy McGrath. It was Donnelly who said he lent James his rifle so that he could go for a smoke, but again this was not corroborated, because McGrath said he was behind the guard hut at the time, phoning his girlfriend.

James left no note. Everyone who knew him was stunned by his death, and his parents remain convinced it was not suicide.

Besides this tragic mystery the death raises important questions, of which the first relates to Surrey Police. They were on the spot promptly and in number, and for the first time in this series of deaths they 'asserted primacy' over the military police.

The detective in charge, however, Inspector Simon Humphreys, did not visit the scene on the night but spoke to officers there by phone. Consequently, as he admitted at the inquest, he was unaware of the Gray death very near the same spot six months earlier. If he had turned up he would almost certainly have been told about it.

Humphreys decided James's death was insufficiently suspicious to merit a full post-mortem: it was carried out by a carried out by a hospital pathologist, rather than a forensic specialist. No blood-spatter photographs were taken either. Nor did anyone ever check the clothing of McGrath or Donnelly, or anyone else, for marks or blood.

Four months passed before a full statement was taken from a corporal who was both one of the last to speak to James (a friendly, relaxed chat) and one of the first to the death scene. As for Private McGrath, he made a very short statement on the night, but it seems to have taken six weeks to get back to him for a proper account.

And though the scene was supposedly thoroughly searched, a cap badge that was almost certainly James's was found in a second search eight months later.

But if Surrey Police failed to cover themselves in glory, neither did the Army. In terms of the events of the night, it turned out that the record in the guardroom log was 'non-contemporaneous' – composed later – while it had to be admitted that there was no record at all of who had been issued with which guns on the night.

Though in some ways the inquest into James's death was a more exacting affair than Nicholas Blake's review – and than the three previous inquests – it was not remotely comprehensive or conclusive. Inquests have limited remits, so army policy and police conduct were never explored, and John Cooper, counsel for the Collinson family, was repeatedly prevented from exploring avenues the family thought important. This was why the coroner himself endorsed calls for a public inquiry.

WHO'S TO BLAME
J'accuse...nobody at all

In the opening pages of his review, Nicholas Blake quotes with approval some words of Des James, the father of Cheryl James, summarising the concerns of the Deepcut families: 'Everything comes back to accountability and confidence that whatever corrective actions are in place...prevent a recurrence'.

However, Blake's report fails in the very matter of accountability. For him, no individual is to blame.

No matter how dreadfully things went wrong at Deepcut, no one is held to account. Never once does Blake say: 'This person, who was paid by the taxpayer to do a job, failed in his duty', or 'That person, who made that decision, must assume responsibility for what followed'.

Official inquiries routinely apportion blame and Blake's remit allowed him to do the same yet he did not do so.

A public inquiry should consider the following.

Deepcut was a blunder from the day in 1993 when the army hurriedly merged three strands of training – standard recruit training, training for women and training for under-17s (you can enlist at 16 years and 9 months) – into one.

A new training programme was also introduced. It began in familiar style with 12 hectic weeks of basic training, known as Phase 1, but then followed a half-baked arrangement, Phase 2, in which trainees waited around while the army tried to arrange courses for them and, eventually, posted them to their final units.

In the Royal Logistics Corps – a unit which, because of its unglamorous character, tends to get the weaker recruits – Phase 2 meant Deepcut. From 1993 on, therefore, about a thousand trainees passed through Deepcut per year, more than a quarter of them women and many of them still 17. Just out of school, away from home for the first time and of mixed abilities (illiteracy was a big problem), they were dumped in Deepcut with not enough to do and no clear idea where they were going.

To cap it all, Deepcut was under-staffed and under-funded at the outset, and was soon subjected to swingeing cuts. A properly staffed modern training establishment has one member of staff to 38 recruits. Through 1995–2002 Deepcut at best had a ratio of one to 60, with one to 100 common. The ratio at night, when many of the staff went home, could reach one to 300.

Such were the essential ingredients of the Deepcut scandal, in which a public institution failed outrageously in its Duty of Care to the vulnerable young people in its charge. Who was responsible for mixing this deadly cocktail?

Nicholas Blake never even asked, but here are some candidates: **Sir Malcolm Rifkind** was Defence Secretary in 1992–5, and **Sir Jeremy Hanley** was his Armed Forces Minister, pushing through drastic cuts in costs. The head of the army was **Field Marshal Sir Peter Inge.** All three should be asked for explanations.

And below them? The documents, if we could see them, must show which soldiers and civil servants wrote the key restructuring recommendations. Blake didn't, but a public inquiry could find them and ask why they exposed teenage volunteers to such risk.

But it wasn't all about policy failure: there were people managing Deepcut in 1995–2002. Blake emphasises how 'challenging' this was, but did they rise to the challenge? He never says.

Off the radar

A key figure is **Lieutenant Colonel Nigel Josling**, commanding officer in 1995, when Sean Benton and Cheryl James died. This was a time of bullying and arbitrary punishment, of hard drinking – by everyone from 17-year-olds to sergeant-majors – and frequent fighting. Deepcut in darkness, admits Blake, was 'an intimidating place'.

Sexual activity was rampant. One official report found that women trainees 'virtually without exception…were having regular sexual intercourse in barracks', in breach of rules. Men routinely entered women's accommodation and vice versa, also breaking rules. When Deepcut's grounds were raked in preparation for an open day, 800 used condoms were collected. Soldiers were even coming in from other bases to have sex.

The staff shortage probably didn't make much difference here, because quite a few were joining in. NCOs routinely 'fraternised' with trainees, often in women's quarters – serious disciplinary matters – and many allegations later emerged of NCOs abusing their authority to get trainees into bed.

How does Lt Col Josling account for this? 'Not on my radar,' he told Blake – he never noticed and no one told him. Even Blake had trouble swallowing this, but Josling insisted: 'That's exactly the sort of feedback and overview one would get if we had adequate supervisory staff'.

You might think that with so few staff he would get to know them well, but he had no idea about Sergeant 'twin brother' B, Andrew Gavaghan, the alleged bully who was also accused of sexual harassment. Josling thought he was 'quite caring, quite imaginative'.

When it comes to what he did to make things better at Deepcut, Josling seems to have been a victim of poor record-keeping. He wanted guard duty reformed, he told Blake, but Blake found no paperwork to confirm this. He complained about staff shortages, he said, but those letters are lost. And he set up a 'risk register' after Sean Benton's death, but no papers survive.

And he doesn't get much help from his boss at the time, **Brigadier Paul Evans**. It was Evans who, after Cheryl James's death, took it upon himself to write what became known as the Evans Report, listing reforms needed to prevent further deaths. By Josling's own account, Evans thought the Deepcut management in 1995 showed inertia, inflexibility and lack of imagination.

Blake never criticises Josling, who has since been promoted.

He left Deepcut early in 1996, to be replaced by **Lieutenant Colonel David Harding**, said by a senior subordinate to have been 'significantly tighter' on discipline. Before long no fewer than three majors were moved on, and Blake notes that Harding's 'interview book' – seeing people who are in trouble – was far thicker than Josling's.

But Harding and his boss, **Brigadier Tony Dalby-Welsh** (Evans too had moved on), turn out to be poor judges of character. Take Lieutenant C, another alleged sexual predator: Though Evans had advised against, Dalby-Welsh 'strongly' recommended him for a new contract in 1996. When C got that contract he moved to a different base, where an outraged commanding officer was soon complaining about his 'falsehoods', 'crass mismanagement' and 'arrogant and cavalier behaviour'. Whoops!

Far worse, though, is the case of Leslie Skinner, a 34-year-old soldier transferred to Deepcut in 1996 after picking up a conviction for flashing at a teenage boy in Northern Ireland. (It was his third such offence.) Harding assigned Skinner to, of all places, the gym, where, incredibly, he worked alongside another convicted sex offender. And months later, when Skinner was offered a transfer to Middlesbrough, Harding effectively endorsed his request to stay at Deepcut.

Whitewash won't wash

Throughout, Skinner was sexually assaulting teenage soldiers who used the gym, and when one of them complained, according to Blake, he was denounced on parade as 'gay' by a sergeant major. Though Skinner was reported and an investigation began, he remained at Deepcut another six months.

What does Blake have to say? Deepcut had a 'difficult task' dealing with Skinner, and the story is 'remarkable', 'difficult to understand' and, at its worst, 'inexplicable'.

But Blake criticises no one – not the unnamed officer who posted a sex offender to a training barracks, not the lieutenant colonel who assigned him to the gym, not the sergeant major who intimidated his accuser, not the Military Police officers who uncovered only a fraction of his offences, and not the unnamed author of the subsequent army whitewash. No one was to blame.

Meanwhile, what was being done to ensure that there was no repeat of the Benton and James affairs? Harding read the Evans report and acted on it so far as he could, beefing up welfare provision, but Evans's main recommendations were not in his power to implement.

Evans wanted professional military guards used at the barracks, to ease the burden of long, boring and lonely assignments on young trainees and, in particular, to reduce the opportunity for them to shoot themselves. And he also urged the army to increase staffing at Deepcut so that trainees could be kept more active and supervised more effectively, with a better chance of spotting those at risk. Both suggestions were meant to save lives. Both implied extra spending. Neither was adopted.

In 1996–8, further reports pointed out that the suicide rate in the army was twice that of the civilian population, also higher than the other armed services, and that the commonest method was gunshot. Again they recommended caution about giving vulnerable teenage recruits access to guns. Again though, nothing was done. Blake's verdict: '*It is a concern* that this continued to be overlooked'.

Out of control

Dalby-Welsh and Harding insist they pressed their bosses at the Army Training and Recruitment Agency (ATRA) for more staff and were rebuffed, though the record on this is thin. Blake remarks that it was only a matter of luck that no one died in this period.

When a new brigadier, **Tweedie Brown,** arrived in 1999 he protested more vigorously to ATRA about staff-trainee ratios, then at one corporal to 120 trainees, or 10 times the army standard. Staff were struggling to cope with disciplinary problems, illiteracy and an outbreak of sexually transmitted disease – more than a hundred trainees were infected.

Brown's complaints were going to the ATRA boss, **Major General Andrew Palmer**, and his response was simple: 'We have no alternative but to manage ATRA business within the resource restrictions imposed on us'. In other words, stop bleating and get on with it. So how were things at Deepcut? Here is a description of the camp in 2001, by a sergeant who worked elsewhere but knew it well: 'Deepcut was run by the recruits. It was out of control. No control at all. After working hours it was like Glasgow or London on a Saturday night. This was every night. For example at the disco at the NAAFI mid-week. Recruits were completely drunk. Both sexes. Staff would be needed to stop fights... There was a party atmosphere.'

By mid-2001 the commanding officer was **Lieutenant Colonel Ron Laden,** who would later accept that he was in charge of a 'sink regiment'. Described as 'of crusading spirit', Laden cracked down on sexual activity and drinking so firmly that ATRA was worried he was too harsh, and he got rid of several errant NCOs. He also pushed staff into keeping trainees busier, to such an extent that some NCOs became ill from overwork.

But the real problems were still ones he could not solve: six years after the Evans Report there were still not nearly enough staff, and armed guard duty was still exposing trainees to unacceptable risk.

What was ATRA doing? General Palmer had stirred himself to commission **Lieutenant Colonel Richard Haes** to study Duty of Care and supervisory ratios across the whole of army training. Haes reported in April 2001, just as Laden arrived at Deepcut.

'The system is failing,' he warned. 'The current situation is tenable only as long as there is no major incident or complaint.' ATRA needed 330 more staff, of which 62 should go to Deepcut, and it must also make much more effort to identify at-risk groups and must use professional military guards.

Here was a direct echo of the 1995 Evans Report – and again none of it was adopted.

General Palmer has since tried to rubbish the Haes report as impractical and Blake has concluded that Palmer never referred to the problems of staffing and guarding upwards to his superiors or ministers. Despite warnings from Haes and others, in other words, he never even asked for more money. Palmer's explanation for this is remarkable.

What with Bosnia, Kosovo, Sierra Leone and foot and mouth, he told a Commons committee, the army was heavily committed in these years, and the front line was very short of men. 'There was significant risk operationally in the Field Army at that time. In order to look at these risks and how to mitigate their effects, a study was undertaken to see whether or not the support organisation – which includes the training organisation – could help reduce the undermanning... About 250 people were moved out of the training organisation into the front line... Essentially... this was an attempt to balance the various risks which existed.'

So, far from increasing the training staff, as the reports urged and the Deepcut commander demanded, the army was reducing it, and Palmer accepted this as a calculated risk. If there were no professional guards at Deepcut, if there was no suicide risk assessment, and if there was inadequate supervision, *that was a matter of official policy.*

Palmer's gamble

Soon after the Haes report was shelved Geoff Gray died at Deepcut – an unsupervised trainee on guard duty with a firearm. And six months after that so did James Collinson.

What does Palmer think of his gamble now? Blake tells us that even with the benefit of hindsight, Palmer told him he would not have acted differently. But Palmer told the Commons committee something different: 'It was all a matter of trying to balance the risk and in so doing... I accept completely that we got that wrong.'

What is Blake's verdict? What does he have to say about the policy decision that exposed teenage trainees to risk in defiance of a whole string of warnings? This: 'The review does not pretend to be able to form a judgement on the competing demands for resources that the defence budget must inevitably face.' In other words, if the army is taking such a huge gamble, who is Blake to question it?

Palmer was promoted to Deputy Chief of the Defence Staff and given a CBE. He has since retired. He would be a key witness at a public inquiry.

After James Collinson's death and the media coverage that resulted, something miraculous happened. Where two deaths had brought no change and three deaths was still not too many, four deaths did the trick: soon staff were flooding into Deepcut, and so were professional guards.

ATRA, however, accepted no blame, its internal inquiry recording merely that the 'guarding regime at Deepcut *inadvertently* created an extraordinarily high level of opportunity risk'. Inadvertently? We can only wonder. The man who wrote that, a **Major General Charlton-Weedy,** should justify it to a public inquiry.

As for Nicholas Blake, the very worst that he can find to say about the army's conduct over the whole Deepcut affair is that it was 'disappointing'. *Disappointing?*

DEEPCUT: THE CONCLUSIONS

Over... and out?

Despite its shortcomings, the Blake report did come up with a series of important recommendations. With the exception of the last (saying there was no need for a public inquiry), the other 33 were meant to help lift the veil of secrecy over the fate of the four recruits and ensure that others like them are no longer exposed to such risks.

So how have they gone down? Some had already been implemented, so won't make any difference. But, worryingly, the most important have been rejected by the government, the army and the Police:

- Ministers rejected Blake's demand for a fully independent ombudsman to investigate complaints – instead opting for a 'service complaints commissioner' who would merely monitor the usual chain of command.

- The government has rejected the request that those under 17 should be trained in separate units from adults.
- It has rejected the suggestion that recruits must have reached the age of 18 before being sent to join field units.
- It has rejected the recommendation that trainees can only carry out armed guard duties under supervision; it remains the case that 17-year-olds may still carry guns on guard duty providing they are not alone.
- Unhappy under-18-year-olds will not, as Blake suggests, be able to leave the army as of right.
- There will not be any automatic disciplinary action against anyone who fails to report bullying or abuse as recommended.
- Neither will complaints of mistreatment, bullying and harassment be automatically investigated by the Royal Military Police – the lesser ones will still go through the chain of command.
- The government has rejected Blake's call for automatic legal aid for families so they can get legal advice or representation at inquests or fatal accident inquiries.
- The MoD has rejected his recommendation that the family be able to attend an army Board of Inquiry into a death and see all the evidence presented to it.
- And finally – despite the recommendation from Blake that the families be given access to all the Police reports and all the supporting evidence and witness statements gathered by them – neither the Surrey reports nor the Devon & Cornwall report have been handed over.

So what was the point of spending nearly £1 million on the Blake review, other than to silence criticism? No new witness was interviewed, let alone cross-examined. Gaping anomalies and inconsistencies remain.

We know that Deepcut was at times out of control, with vulnerable young trainees exposed to risks their parents could not have imagined, and we know more about the bullying, sex, drink, and the flouting of rules – notably those concerning firearms.

What we don't have are accounts of the four deaths in which we can see that the evidence and the witnesses have been challenged and the anomalies have been confronted rather than ducked. We don't have nearly sufficient assurances that where the army and police have made changes they will stick. And we don't have any evidence of accountability at work – pretty well everyone involved, apart from the four recruits themselves (and Leslie Skinner, who went to jail), has escaped sanction of any kind, so far as we know.

Blake's review was built on poor foundations, since it relied almost unquestioningly on a re-investigation by the same police force which made the fundamental errors after the bodies were found. Because both the Surrey Police findings and the Devon & Cornwall report are secret, no one can judge their quality. Even the expert reports are withheld, when the whole point of expert evidence is that it should be peer-tested.

Article two of the European Convention on Human Rights provides that where someone has died who is under the care of the state – a thorough and independent inquiry with the participation of the family must take place.

None of the Police inquiries, or the inquests, or the Defence Committee investigation or Blake's review, meets that standard. Even the coroner at the end of James Collinson's inquest added his weight to the demands for a public inquiry. That is the only way out of the tragic mess of the Deepcut affair.

Appendix B2

Deepcut: The media messed up
By Brian Cathcart

Published in the British Journalism Review, *Vol 18, No.1, 2007.*

In spring 2002, researchers from the BBC television programme Frontline Scotland stumbled across what would become a very big story. They were looking into the mysterious death by shooting of James Collinson, a young army recruit from Perth, and they had already established that a strikingly similar death had occurred at the same Surrey barracks where Collinson died, just six months earlier. Then they made their big discovery: there had been not just two such deaths at the barracks, but four. Two young soldiers had died there in 1995, also by gunshot, and also in unexplained circumstances. So began the scandal of Deepcut.

No great insight is required to see why that discovery made it a big story: two may be a coincidence, but four is something else. Four young people (two of them aged just 17) were dead, leaving four grieving families, and no one could, or would, say why they had died (although in one case an inquest had recorded a suicide verdict, the finding was contested, not least because the soldier was shot five times). The possibilities were alarming. Had they been murdered? Was there a serial killer? Were the deaths, whether murders or not, the results of extreme bullying? How had the Army permitted four such similar deaths to occur? And why did the fact that there had been four deaths have to be ferreted out by journalists, rather than being placed on the record by the Army? The testimony of the families only increased the alarm. Officers had seemed remarkably keen, even before any investigations had taken place, to convince them the deaths were suicides. Inquests had been brisk affairs, evidence had been lost or destroyed and there was a powerful smell of cover-up.

Today, five years on, there is a general perception that the Deepcut scandal is over. Many people are under the impression that a proper inquiry has been conducted and that it found that the deaths were suicides. And besides, the affair has been crowded out by Iraq and Afghanistan, which have thrown up a raft of other concerns about the Army. Though the Deepcut families have not given up, editors are now loath to commission articles about the affair; they believe, in rough terms, that it is now history. This represents a triumph for the Ministry of Defence, which in five years never rested in its efforts to kill a story that it would have preferred we had never known about.

This is not the place to explore the arguments about what went wrong at Deepcut and why. Instead I would like, as someone who has reported the case from a fairly early stage, to make an observation about the contribution of journalists. Despite considerable difficulties, journalists did pretty well in pushing the story forward and unearthing new information, though it was always the bereaved families who drove the story. But then I believe we were outmanoeuvred by the Ministry of Defence, tricked if you like, into letting the matter drop. It was a simple trick and I'm not sure what we could have done about it, but I think at least we should recognise that it happened.

Withheld from the public

A little background: after the scandal broke, for 15 months, the Government was able to keep a lid on the Deepcut affair by simple means. The Surrey Police, who had botched the investigations of the deaths the first time around (they later apologised), were conducting a re-investigation, and while that was going on ministers systematically refused to comment – the matter was in the hands of the Police. Then, in September 2004, an astonishing thing happened. Surrey Police completed their report, but did not publish it. All they issued was a four-page press release containing the headline statement that they had not found evidence to justify charging anyone. Since that was all there was, it was all that could be reported – a message superficially reassuring for the public but without any evidence on the record to support it. To this day the full report, reputed to be 2,500 pages long, is withheld from the public, and even the legal teams of the victims' families are not allowed to read it.

The Government, now open to questioning, seized upon this fat document, which no journalist or politician outside the loop had seen, and used it as another smokescreen. In the Commons Tony Blair implied that everything possible had been done to unearth the truth. 'There has been a very detailed police investigation of the deaths,' he said, 'with about 900 witnesses being interviewed and 1,500 statements taken over 15 months, and we are grateful to the chief constable of Surrey Police for his report.' (Readers with long memories might recall Richard Nixon's White House using very similar language to impart credibility to a Justice Department investigation which concluded that Watergate was a simple burglary.)

That the Deepcut affair did not run into the sand right there we owe, paradoxically, to the same Surrey Police, who, after burying their report on the deaths, did something both surprising and welcome. In March 2004 they produced an additional report – and this time it was actually published – which opened a new front: it addressed the Army's 'Duty of Care' at the barracks in 1995–2002 and left little doubt that there had been grave failings. A climate existed in Deepcut that presented grave dangers to the young trainees who passed through there, but despite repeated warnings, the Army did not do enough about it. This was what the families, their lawyers and many reporters had come to suspect: the four deaths, terrible as they were, were only a part of the true Deepcut scandal, an extreme symptom of it.

In the months that followed there was widespread outrage, articulated in and fed by revelatory television programmes and newspaper articles, as well as by public evidence to a Commons Select Committee investigation of Army Duty of Care. Perhaps most shocking was the arrest in 2004 of a former Deepcut NCO, Leslie Skinner, who had exploited his authority to sexually abuse male trainee soldiers at the camp (he was later jailed). Despite the efforts of Geoff Hoon, then Defence Secretary, and his Armed Forces Minister Adam Ingram, the scandal would not go away. As the bereaved families drove pressure both within Parliament and outside, ministers looked for a way out.

So was created, in December 2004, the Deepcut Review, conducted by Nicholas Blake QC – and here we are approaching the point where journalism dropped the ball. The Review was conducted behind closed doors over 15 months (once again giving the Government an excuse to bat away awkward questions). It worked entirely behind closed doors, though Blake met the families and persuaded them to co-operate (something they now regret). Then on March 29 last year Blake presented his report (the circumstances were carefully choreographed in that the families were not allowed to speak at the same press conference). It ran to 400 pages, with nearly 2,000 pages of appendices, but coverage of it was dominated by a single newsline: Blake concluded that, on the balance of probabilities, the soldiers had killed themselves. (In fact he dealt with only three deaths, having ruled himself out of commenting on the fourth because the inquest was still pending.) Other angles were covered in the press, in particular some further shocking information about bullying and neglect at Deepcut, but this finding of 'probable suicide' was the key message delivered to the public.

So far as news value was concerned, this was what you might expect. The scandal began, after all, with public alarm about the four deaths; here was a conclusion about three of those deaths by a leading barrister. It was the story. And yet much else of vital importance in the Blake report was missed or obscured, including, in my view, shortcomings grave enough to cast doubt on its credibility. Why did this happen? A simple, mechanical reason: there was just one window of opportunity for reporters to write about the report and they self-evidently did not have the time to digest it. In effect, even though some certainly tried to go deeper, journalists could do little more than relay a soundbite, which happened also to be the one the MoD desperately wanted in the public domain.

Every twist of the case

Nothing unusual about that, you may say. Published reports are frequently long and journalists with deadlines are always under pressure to deal with them rapidly – Hutton, Scott and Macpherson were all reported in a hurry and in those three cases we got the message, didn't we? Perhaps, but Blake was different: it had not been a public inquiry. I know from experience that reporters who follow an inquiry that has weighed evidence in months of open hearings are far better equipped to deal quickly with a long report than they were in the case of Blake. There were dozens of Hutton geeks who knew every twist of the case by the time that report came out, and as a result they were able to identify its weaknesses almost instantly. Not so with

Blake; there are very few Deepcut geeks, and we are characterised by how little we know, rather than how much.

At the very heart of this scandal has been the withholding of information – reporters, families and the public have been kept in the dark – yet Blake worked in secret, reading secret papers and holding secret meetings, before producing a long report, without an index and with voluminous appendices on disk, in which the cast of players was unfamiliar and even, since he chose to identify many of them by letters rather than names, baffling. For those reasons and because of its structure and writing style it was an extremely difficult document to penetrate. It took me weeks to come to a conclusion about the job Blake had done. By then the news agenda had moved on and the public had registered, in a broad-brush way, that the case was closed. With no knowledge based on daily reporting of how Blake's inquiries unfolded, the public could not follow the evolution of the arguments. In my view, at the moment the 400-page outcome was unveiled, most people were still at square one in terms of understanding the issues. It is even true of the families, who knew the issues far better but were given no time to digest the report before its publication.

There is a message here for campaigners: if at all possible, do not accept or co-operate with a behind-closed-doors investigation. There is also an important message for reporters and editors. Governments, when they think they can get away with it, will use this device again. They will spring a mass of information on us in the knowledge that we have no hope of processing it in time to meet that day's deadlines, and they know as we know that the second and third day's coverage rarely makes the front page. We should be alert to this and should try to subvert it as we do all the other devices of spin.

I need to say, briefly, what I think was missed a year ago. In collaboration with Heather Mills, the experienced crime and home affairs correspondent now at *Private Eye*, I eventually wrote a lengthy response to Blake, which appeared as a special report in the *Eye* last September. We concluded that his approach and methods were flawed, that many of his most important findings were not borne out even by the evidence he selected to support them, and that he has not come near to clearing up the circumstances of the deaths. Almost by accident, however, he effectively proved a case of wilful negligence by the army high command, and then let them all off scot-free. A barracks that was supposed to train young soldiers was allowed to become a sewer of abuse and indiscipline over a period of seven years, for no other reason than that senior commanders chose to distribute funding elsewhere. Four deaths made no difference; only when the scandal erupted in public did things change.

I have in my notebook a remarkable quotation from Des James, the father of Cheryl James, killed by gunshot in Deepcut in 1995 at the age of 18. In exasperation at the news fix I have just described, he said to me last summer: 'Was it suicide? Who the hell cares?' He wasn't being callous – far from it. Nor was he adjusting his position because of some change in the evidence about his daughter's death, because that remains as unclear as ever. What he meant was that when you realise the state of affairs in Deepcut, you see that the precise manner of the deaths is almost irrelevant. One way or another young people were bound to die in such a place, and the miracle is that there weren't more deaths. That is the message that went astray because reporters and the public were outwitted. Knowing what we now know (and that is still less than half the picture), we should expect people to be held to account. Nobody has been, because Blake let them all off the hook – but it was impossible to convey such a message in short order last March.

All this may be history now – though the families are pursuing legal routes to a public inquiry – but it is not without current resonance. Deepcut was left to run amok by the Army because resources were tight. Just such a squeeze is under way within the Armed Forces once more today and there is no guarantee that commanders will not make the same, potentially disastrous, decisions again.

Copyright © 2007 Brian Cathcart.
Reprinted with permission.

Appendix C1

Additional verbatim material

FRANK SWANN, independent forensics expert

SURREY POLICE PRESS STATEMENT: 'We have this afternoon formally received details from Mr Swann. There appear to be differences between the findings of Mr Swann, the Forensic Science Service and the German Federal Crime Bureau [known as the BKA]. Mr Swann has agreed to meet other experts to jointly discuss their findings and rationale behind them.' **[E1]**

SWANN: They [Surrey Police] asked us to attend a meeting near Reigate Police Station where the BKA – who have never attended the scenes – the Forensic Science Service and myself and our team were to present to each other our evidence. Now I was all game for that and I agreed to attend. Then they said that it was going to be videoed by the Police and I said 'Well, I'm quite happy for that but we will want our own videographer there and we will videograph the meeting as well because we're not going to have it edited. It's got to be a complete thing of the whole meeting.' Well, the minute we insisted on having our own videographer present, they cancelled the meeting. They wasn't even prepared, if they'd used only them, to give us a copy of it immediately onto a computer. Why would they cancel? They didn't want us to be in possession of what everybody else said 'cause if it went into the public domain even Joe Brown who knows nothing about forensics would have known that it was nonsense. I don't think it's going to die. It might go quiet but as soon as somebody gets killed or something happens over here, you know, look how it blows up when something happens. So, sooner or later somebody – maybe genuine – in politics or something will come along and decide. But you see what I do hope to some extent is that the Government will change and that somebody will say 'Let's have a good look at this. Let's see and produce all the evidence.' There might be evidence where I'm wrong and [others] are right – but the only way we're going to do it is all get in a room and go through it, together. But if they're going to video it, I want a copy. **[V]**

Appendix C2

Additional verbatim material

MAJOR (RETD.) ECCLES, Former Army Officer

The situation is that I know nothing of what happened at Deepcut after Options for Change because I'd already decided to leave the sinking ship. What I can give you is probably the broadest and most in depth knowledge of someone who served at Blackdown as [Deepcut] was called. I first went to school there in 1954. I was four. My father was posted there and went to Suez from Blackdown. In fact, he never got there because the war was so short. [He] returned [to Blackdown] in 1967 as Deputy Commander of the whole of the complex and I came back and lived at Blackdown as a teenager. In 1968, I joined the Army at 18. I'd always planned to join because I saw my father have his career and he'd always had a good time and there was plenty of sport and I thought, 'Boy, this is the life for me'. I also liked the Regimental family aspect that the Army always engendered. You joined not only 'To Serve King and Country' but to be together with the other people you served with. So, 68, I sign up but I didn't have Maths O-level and you're saying 'What the hell's this got to do with it?' Because I hadn't got Maths O level I had to join as a private soldier. Guess where I was posted? [I did my basic training at] Blackdown barracks. I was kitted up and I went into my first barracks. We lived twenty men to a room, bunkbeds, end of the room, you went into a little corridor, on the left hand side lived the lance corporal and on the right hand side lived the corporal – looking after twenty of us. That was the ratio, you see. I then did two years at Sandhurst and I came back to Blackdown for my Junior Officer's training. So, I'd been a little boy at Blackdown then I'd seen it as a young man and then I actually join and go into a barrack room. I go through Sandhurst, I pass out and I join the RAOC – Royal Army Ordnance Corps. [It's all changed now] – it's the Really Large Corps – sorry, the Royal Logistics Corps. (*Laughs.*)

Blackdown was basically Ordnance's main training centre. Ordnance has all those different trades which are vital to keeping any Army going – storemen, drivers, clerical support – the store and supply of all storage items. [There were] no women being trained as soldiers at Blackdown at that time. It's huge – basically the training that happened in Blackdown covered all the aspects of being an Ordnance Corps officer/soldier. The other specialisation was vehicles – the storage and supply of all vehicles to the Army and also food technology which is the supply and quality control of all food items coming into the Army. So it was a huge, huge depot with this great variety of jobs that you could do. And it's one of the reasons that I spent very nearly half my twenty five year career there.

Until Options for Change, Ordnance ran very much along traditional regimental lines. You have a Colonel, you have a 2IC, you have a Regimental Headquarters which is responsible for your three companies and each company is supposed to be a hundred men and every company had three platoons and they're 30 men and each platoon has ten men sections and in charge of each section is a corporal and you have a sergeant in charge of the three corporals and an officer in charge of them all. So, you have this hierarchical structure where everybody is looking, keeping an eye out for everybody else. A ratio of 1:10 – the ratio there sometimes went up to 1:20 but these were trained soldiers now doing their employment training so they were one step along and they weren't there for that long but it was still 1:20 which was just about OK. So, even Ordnance maintained that traditional military hierarchical system throughout its existence up to that period, the Options for Change.

In those early years, the only furore I can remember – the only death ever recorded at Blackdown was when a young lad from the Apprentice College went – obviously, a number of them – went skinny dipping and one lad drowned. And that was simply bad luck. That was an accident. The reason I mention it is because it was a memorable accident. He shouldn't have died and the swimming pool was subsequently fenced off to stop easy access but nevertheless it was a death for which people were quite agitated because you don't like to lose anybody. You have a Duty of Care to those people. My father felt it very strongly when that lad died.

I'm not saying there was no bullying in those years. There was, of course, bullying. There are always elements in any – especially male-dominated – environment that are easy targets and for some reason or other it's just, you know, human nature to pick on people. But it was a family environment – you had the NAAFI, the – you know, the Army sort of club where you could go drinking at subsidised prices – inevitably people who lived and worked on and around the base worked in there and they would keep an eye on things. And there was also a padre and there was a little more religion in those days and people would feel that they could go and talk to the padre. And then you had the WRVS as well, [the] Women's Volunteer Service and they were a refuge where people who had problems could go. So, it had all these levels of care. Because you have a responsibility of care for those young people. To them and to their parents.

If someone was identified as being unsuitable there was absolutely no problem about getting rid of them. You just have them in and you talk to them. Some were disappointed, some were just medical problems. There was also the mental side – most of the people we discharged because they were mentally unsuitable, understood that they were mentally unsuitable and went. There were very few that we discharged who were aggrieved by being discharged. Obviously, there will [have been] people who wanted to get out but it wasn't nearly as prevalent in our day because it was a family organisation and you joined it as a young soldier, male or female, and there was a good bit of camaraderie and it's something that when you're 16 to 25 you actually quite enjoyed doing. Not everybody and yes there were people who said, 'Oh, well, I don't like it', but the proportion was so small that it really didn't matter if they were adamant that they wanted to go. Basically, you made it a bit hard for them and then if you saw they wanted to go, you just let them go.

My feeling always was that women should be allowed to join the Army freely and unhindered and allowed to join whatever they are capable of doing. It's divisive to have an organisation where you have a woman soldier and a man soldier – the man soldier has to do ten press ups and the woman only has to do five, the man has to run three miles and the woman two. I mean, the point is there are a lot of strong, effective women out there who can do ten press ups and can run three miles. And a lot of men that can't. If they want to be an infantry soldier, let them be an infantry soldier. All this crap about where are they going to pee and are the men going to take advantage of them? They are not going to take advantage of them and if they are you will find that they will be slapped down by the other lads because the forces until recently was always an organisation that looked after its own and if you had a woman come into the unit and she is a good soldier and the lads liked her, if one lad tried to take advantage of her, the other lads would knock him down.

Later on when I was at Blackdown as the 2IC of the training battalion we were then getting women soldiers in as well and we kept them segregated. There was a woman's block and the lads' block and I argued, completely unsuccessfully, that they should be mixed. Don't segregate them. Put the men and women together and they will all be better for it because the men will look after the women, the men will dress better, behave better, get less drunk, and the same will happen with the women. That is slightly simplistic. There obviously would be problems that you would have to meet anyway because there are always rogue elements. It's not going to stop the man bursting into the women's block and it didn't stop the men going into the women's block and trying to 'have it away'. It would have saved some of the broken legs we had though. Jumping out [of windows]. We used to go into the women's blocks and someone would keep a look out and then he would say, 'Look out, Duty Officer' and all these lads would be jumping out of the windows and crawling away with broken legs.

Guard duty was just something you did that was a bit shitty because it was done throughout the night and at weekends. I was talking to my friend who was a corporal at the height of the [IRA] troubles. He was a Guard Commander and he would take out the patrols that went round the perimeter fences. He never indicated that it was unbearable, it was just a duty that had to be done and it wasn't done that often. It's a good way of punishing people as well cause it was a bit shitty so if someone needed a quick and simple punishment you gave them a couple of extra guard duties.

On the few occasions that Blackdown was actually threatened [my friend] can remember only issuing ammunition twice. The ammunition was kept in the safe and often you didn't bother with the weapon, you just took a club out. 'Cause it's easier to wield a club than an empty [rifle]. The ammunition is in a magazine [and] in time of imminent threat those magazines would be issued to the Guard Commander out of a safe by the Duty Officer and they were counted out and they were counted back in again and woe betide anybody who lost a single round. They were given to each man who put it in his pocket – not on the rifle, in the pocket – until they came under fire. Then the chap leading the patrol would have got them to put the live ammunition onto the weapon. But until such time as they were being fired upon or about to be fired upon, those weapons were never loaded. My friend remembers issuing ammunition twice; I only ever remember the order being given once. And the ammunition was never loaded onto a weapon.

The deaths at Deepcut actually came as – as quite a surprise to me when eventually it filtered through. I was stunned. I thought, 'How can that happen?' I'd done all that time since 1954 to '92 with two deaths, three deaths – the one in the swimming pool when my father was at the Apprentice College; one lad when I was in the Training Battalion as a 2IC who went on a run, fell over and stopped breathing. They took him to hospital, opened him up and he had a hole in his heart. There was not a hint anywhere that it was anything other than a morning run, which it was. Just a normal morning run. And an officer fell down stairs in mysterious circumstances in his quarters but he was suffering from terminal cancer and they felt that it was an accident. So, to find that there had been four deaths in Deepcut since I'd left – from gunshot wounds –

The Commanding Officer at Deepcut shouldn't allow ammunition to be issued, these deaths happened basically when the threat to mainland military bases, which the IRA seldom attacked, was over. So, why do those lads need to be armed? And lass? Why were they allowed to go off unaccompanied? Armed and unaccompanied? I'd have been scared stiff if my guards had had live ammunition! Simply because accidents happen – forgetting to put the safety catch on or loading or something – accidents happen and it can do a lot of damage.

There is no question about primacy. It is absolutely and utterly laid down. In peacetime, the Police have primacy over all serious incidents in military barracks in Great Britain. And I'm not just talking about [a] death; I'm talking about if there's a serious injury. The police should be called in and they should investigate. But there will always be doubt in those parents' minds over actually how [their children] died and if the Police had been able to carry out proper forensic tests, they could have said, 'It's beyond doubt'. Instead of following laid-down procedures those involved simply appeared to panic.

I wouldn't have been happy being sent to Blackdown and I certainly would not have asked to go to Blackdown in the current regime, knowing that I was basically a caretaker. You would just hope that nothing shitty happened on your watch, because you wanted your career to be unblemished, so you would definitely avoid being sent to Blackdown if you could. One of the problems with that is you then get people that regiments want to 'move on,' so you're likely to end up with some second rate officers and NCOs who don't want to be there. This is unfair to many and, of course, only conjecture.

[The father of James Collinson] phoned up and said 'Look, I've been put onto you by one of [your] NCOs who said, "If you want to know anything about Deepcut, ask Eccles 'cause I know he's been there forever".' [He] was desperate to prove his son was killed. But I said to [Mr] Collinson, 'Look, you are chasing the wrong target. Don't chase the Police and the military system for allowing your son to be killed by a third party. Chase them for allowing them to fall down on the Duty of Care.' I tried my very best to get him to understand that point. Because the bottom line is that even if it was a third party that killed his son, it wouldn't have happened if the Duty of Care had been carried out properly, in that, he wasn't given a loaded weapon and allowed to patrol with a loaded weapon on his own. So, whatever the outcome his son's death would have been vindicated in that he would have helped to stop future deaths happening because the military system would have had to have seen the error of it's ways, of taking an organisation with a ratio of 1:10 and turning it into 1:60, which doesn't work. However their children were killed the Government are ultimately responsible for not making sure that the safety nets were all in position. That's why their sons and Cheryl died, because the people weren't there to look after them anymore.

I'm sad that Blackdown which was the home of the RAOC became the Princess Royal Barracks at Deepcut [where] four people have been killed. I'm sad that the military system has been allowed to deteriorate so badly that it should be able to happen. Many more have died at Catterick so it is just a sign of the times which makes it even sadder that our Armed Forces have been allowed to deteriorate so badly. It needn't have deteriorated so fast and so far as it has done. The government 'pen-pushers' and money-savers are steadily destroying the traditions of the British Army as I knew it. But times move on, I know. [V]

Appendix C3

Additional verbatim material

LEMBIT ÖPIK MP

DES: Lembit Öpik was the one who started it politically and that's the most amazing thing of all really. MPs take a lot of flack but I mean, I didn't ring him, I didn't ask for help. He rang me…

ÖPIK: It was highlighted to me that Des James lived in my constituency and that the Deepcut Army barracks issue was highly contentious. That something had happened there which hadn't been fully explained. I got in touch with [him] on the phone and said, 'Look, I'm very interested in this and if you want me to help, I will help'. At that time I had no idea that the ripples on the surface lead to very, very strong currents beneath the surface.

On the Devon & Cornwall Police report into Surrey Police's investigations:

I have attempted to use the Freedom of Information Act to get this information because after all what could be more in line with natural justice than giving the parents of the deceased the chance to look at a report into an investigation of how the deaths of their kids were looked into? But does Des James have the right to look at it? Apparently not. If [Surrey Police] had put the amount of energy they've spent on refusing to disclose information into the original investigation, maybe Des and Doreen James would have found out what happened to their kid reliably eleven years ago. But instead the word 'suicide' is used time and again by the authorities to give the impression that this was necessarily suicide. Now to Des and Doreen's eternal credit, they have never said that they know it isn't suicide. All they have said is they don't know that it was and they can't see why anybody else should claim it was when the evidence hasn't even been shared with them. Sorry, I'm pretty annoyed about the whole thing. Makes you wonder now, who actually do the Police [and] the Army work for? Who pays them? The same people who pay MPs like me. The public. I get the feeling sometimes the authorities in these institutions have forgotten that and they think in some ways they have the right to tell the public what they are allowed to know. Actually, accepting there sometimes need to be confidences, it's beyond me why anyone can seriously think that either the credibility of the Police or their operational effectiveness is in any way helped or protected by the failure to disclose information, which in itself would help us improve the operational effectiveness of the Police and the Army. It just looks like people protecting themselves. Or worse.

DES: [Lembit] won an adjournment debate and I went down for that. You know, I've always been interested in politics and I think in the adjournment debate there was a realisation that you're not just facing the MoD. You're facing the establishment. [V]

Speech by Lembit Öpik MP at Westminster Hall adjournment debate on Deepcut, 27th April 2004. Source: Hansard.

LEMBIT ÖPIK

I am extremely grateful for the opportunity to discuss this issue in an Adjournment debate, and I thank the Minister of State, Ministry of Defence, for his constructive approach in the run-up to the debate. I know that the timing of today's debate was exceedingly difficult for him, because of other unmoveable commitments – in Afghanistan, I think – so I am extremely grateful to the Secretary of State for Defence for agreeing to respond today. That is generally appreciated. In that spirit I assure him that my aim is not to find villains in the Department, but to find answers. I am increasingly optimistic that answers can be found in partnership with the Ministry of Defence.

I am asking for an independent public inquiry into the four unexplained deaths at the Princess Royal Barracks at Deepcut in Surrey. Between 1995 and 2002, four soldiers died at Deepcut: Private Sean Benton died on 9 June 1995, Private Cheryl James died on 27 November 1995, Private Geoff Gray died on 21 September 2001 and Private James Collinson died on 23 March 2002. All were members of the Royal Logistic Corps and were in phase 2 training. All died from gunshot wounds.

The first three deaths were investigated by Surrey Police and inquests were held. Open verdicts were given in the cases of Privates James and Gray. The Surrey coroner's opinion was that Private Benton took his own life. Private Benton was shot five times, Private Gray was shot twice and Privates James and Collinson were found with one gunshot wound each. During their investigations into Private Collinson's death, Surrey Police decided to reopen the three previous cases. The report on the deaths went to the Surrey coroner on 19 September 2003 and a further report was published on March 4 2004 outlining the Police's concerns about the apparent lack of safeguards built into the Army's care regime and about wider cultural and organisational issues in the Army. The police called for a broader enquiry.

I shall illustrate the case for that inquiry through the example of the late Cheryl James. Cheryl was the daughter of my constituents Des and Doreen James. She died, as I said, on 27 November 1995. In our view, to this day her death remains unexplained. Cheryl died armed and alone, guarding an internal gate. She should never have been armed and alone. Army regulations state: 'Servicewomen may be armed and employed on the same basis as adult male soldiers. The only proviso is that, where possible, armed Servicewomen should be accompanied by male personnel. If this is not possible, Servicewomen are to be employed in "pairs".' To the Board of

Inquiry, the Army admitted that 'the unit was mistaken in believing it could employ Servicewomen, armed and alone, on guard duties'.

It also acknowledged that recruits are not made aware of those regulations during phase 1 or phase 2 training, so the onus is very much on the Army to ensure that the regulations are observed. Despite the clear-cut guidance and the evident breach, the Army found that it was not culpable. The matter could not be clearer: Cheryl was armed and alone when she died, which was clearly contrary to regulations.

On further inspection, we find that, prior to Cheryl's death and afterwards, Army procedure and regulations were flouted again and again. The Army did not insist that Surrey Police adopt primacy for the investigation into the death. The special investigation branch did not mark off the scene to prevent evidence being destroyed or lost; the barracks was not stood down and closed to those arriving or leaving, contrary to stated Army procedure following a death. No ballistic evidence was taken, so one cannot be sure that the bullet found in Cheryl came from her SA80 rifle: there is no evidence to ensure conclusively the connection between the weapon and the death. Amazingly, it seems that the bullet was recovered and then lost. A witness who attended the post-mortem alleged that the bullet was put into a specimen jar and then discarded. The list goes on, and none of those actions have been accounted for. Was it incompetence, negligence or cover-up? Furthermore, one cannot know whether the Ministry of Defence officers who investigated Cheryl's death are still operating in the same manner today.

The details regarding Cheryl's death only emerged from the Surrey Police re-investigation completed in September 2003. That alone would warrant an independent inquiry into her death, but it is just the start. The day Cheryl died an Army officer from a local barracks in Wrexham informed Mr and Mrs James of their daughter's death. He told them that Cheryl had 'taken her own life' but could not answer any further questions. The James were not contacted by any Army or Ministry of Defence official between her death on 27 November and her funeral on 4 December. After that, the James had no Army or MoD contact– official or otherwise–for seven years, and then did so only as a result of the Surrey Police investigation.

Back in 1995, Mr and Mrs James did not feel like questioning the facts. They felt isolated and distressed about the way in which the Army handled their daughter's death. Understandably, the lack of compassion was underlined when some of her property was returned by courier and the driver – not knowing any better – merely got the James to sign for what felt like their daughter's life, as one would sign for office supplies. Some items, such as her mobile phone, were missing – her belongings had evidently become separated. Things were randomly posted back to Mr and Mrs James, pretty much out of the blue with no explanation, marked simply 'the late Cheryl James', and the James still do not know if everything was returned. Such insensitivity in the approach of the Ministry of Defence and the Army to bereaved families sadly continues. Reg Keys, whose son Lance Corporal Thomas Keys died in Iraq on 24 June 2003, reported experiencing the same attitude of indifference and lack of transparency just one month ago. Time and time again, grieving families are left to wait and wonder.

Surrey Police acknowledged the shortcomings of the original investigations into the four deaths. They apologised to families for not taking the lead in ensuring a thorough inquest at the outset. The Army wrote to Mr and Mrs James to say that it had 'misunderstood the regulations in place at the time'.

In Des and Doreen's own words, they paid a big price for the Army misunderstanding its own regulations. Despite the apparent admission of negligence by the Army, no apology has ever been made and no one ever held accountable for the death of Cheryl James. Above all, and leaving aside their feelings of bereavement, the James still do not know for sure what happened to their daughter.

Four further points underscore and bolster their doubts. First, an independent ballistics expert hired by the families has said that it is 'highly unlikely' that three of the four deaths at Deepcut were self-inflicted. In layman's terms, there may have been third-party involvement. Let us not play around with words: that could mean manslaughter or murder. Regarding Cheryl's death, the expert said that if someone used the SA80 rifle to take their own life, it would be highly unlikely that the bullet was retrieved, as the gun is so powerful. Apparently, however the bullet was retrieved–and disposed of. None of that has been explained. He also said that the pattern of gunshot residue on her hand indicated that she was pushing the gun away from her face.

Secondly, the Army referred to Cheryl's death as suicide both prior to and after the coroner's inquest, despite guidelines saying that: 'it is not for the Army to reach any official conclusion as to the death of any Serviceman or woman; cause of death in such circumstances can only be established by Her Majesty's Coroner following the civilian police investigation and report.'

Thirdly, one week before the coroner's inquest, the Army issued a document referring to Cheryl's death as 'a tragic suicide'. She is even included in the suicide statistics. However, the coroner returned an open verdict. Three weeks after the coroner's inquest, the Army conducted its own so-called Board of Inquiry, which concluded that: 'notwithstanding the Coroner's verdict, it is the opinion of the board that' Private 'James shot herself and that the possibility of her action being accidental is negligible'.

Where is the evidence? The parents have a right to know how and what the Army knows that draws it to that conclusion. Why has the Army never shared the evidence used to back up those claims? Let us note that a member of the Board of Inquiry registered a statement of discontent with the board's verdict. That should ring a loud alarm bell.

Fourthly, the board claimed that Private James 'apparently took six distinct and positive actions in relation to her weapon and ammunition which were clearly beyond her duty at the time, the omission of any one of which would have meant she may not have been killed'.

Here are the six 'distinct and positive actions'. First, she removed a charged magazine of ten rounds from her pocket. How do they know that? Secondly, she placed a charged magazine on her weapon. How do they know that? Thirdly, she cocked the weapon. How do they know that? Fourthly, she released the safety catch. How do they know that? Fifthly, she reversed the weapon so that it was aimed at herself. How do they know that? Sixthly, she pulled the trigger. How do they know that? No witnesses are cited. Where does the information come from? Such contradictions, assumptions and apparently unsupported claims add to the case for an independent public inquiry to resolve the unanswered questions.

Deepcut should want one too. After all, in just 19 weeks, two deaths and ten cases of self-harm were recorded. No questions were asked, but the camp commander was moved just three days after the second death. The commanding officer never phoned or wrote to Mr and Mrs James. Interestingly, last year he was awarded an OBE. He has never been questioned publicly about what happened at the camp. Someone with such a noble record will, I am sure, want to help to clear up the matter, not least because he was responsible for the camp at the time when much of it occurred. Let us note also that the Army's Adjutant-General, Lieutenant General Sir Alistair Irwin, admits, the Army had 'clearly failed' all four Deepcut soldiers, adding, 'they're not now alive and they should be alive'.

However, by saying that Private Benton's death had been the first at Deepcut for 40 years, he defended the Army against police claims that the Army did nothing. After such a long record of calm, should not two deaths in 19 weeks have rung loud alarm bells?

I turn to the Surrey Police report and subsequent comments. While not pushing for a criminal prosecution, they were so concerned about events uncovered in their investigations that they produced a report calling for a broader inquiry. They said that 'the families have, quite rightly, refused to accept the deaths of their children without question'. The police apologised to the four families for not properly challenging early assumptions that these young soldiers took their own lives and for their failure to overturn the then practice of allowing the investigation to be delegated to the Army. The police now recognise that they should have maintained primacy over the Army in the investigation. The civil police now conduct an independent investigation immediately when untimely non-combatant military deaths occur. However, the Police say that 'there remains much more to be done' to 'address areas of risk'.

Furthermore, parents' rights are still not sufficiently respected. For example, Board of Inquiry reports are meant to be passed to the next of kin, but rarely are.

Perhaps that is why the Defence Committee took on board in its Duty of Care inquiry some issues raised by Surrey Police. That is good, but I cannot emphasise enough the admission by the Committee that it simply cannot answer the core questions about the deaths at Deepcut. Incidentally, so that people are not confused, let me make it clear that, although the Committee announced its inquiry on the same day as the final report of Surrey Police was published, the two are not linked. The Committee is looking broadly into all three forces. It is not investigating bullying, harassment, the management of Deepcut when the recruits died or mistakes made during the investigations at Deepcut. The Committee says that it cannot do justice to those matters, and I agree. Only a public inquiry would have the time and resources to generate as definitive an account as is now possible, after the intervening time.

What outcomes would we want from a public inquiry? Surrey Police were concerned about incidents of bullying. That has been a concern of MPs and peers since 1989 and possibly earlier, with numerous parliamentary questions and debates. An inquiry should investigate that issue in relation to Deepcut. An inquiry should also study the high incidence of military suicide. The Defence Analytical Services Agency report of July 2003, entitled 'Suicide and Open Verdict Deaths among males in the UK Regular Armed Forces', found that 'between 1984 and 2002 there were 446 coroner-informed suicides' in the Armed Forces. That is one suicide every fortnight, most – 62 per cent – occurring in the Army. That figure excludes open verdicts and other non-combatant deaths. The important point is that Army males under 20 years old are 50 per cent more likely to be registered as having committed suicide than males under 20 in the UK civilian population. Incidentally, suicide rates among the under-25s are higher in the Army than in the Navy or the Royal Air Force. The DASA report says that the higher suicide rates among young Army males compared with the equivalent UK civilian population merit further investigation. A public inquiry should consider that in the context of Deepcut. I remind right hon. and hon. Members that three of the four deaths at Deepcut were of young males. Above all, a public inquiry should aim to determine what happened at Deepcut. The final report of Surrey Police reinforces the case for thorough, independent scrutiny to establish the circumstances at the time of the Deepcut deaths, plus corrective actions to prevent reoccurrence.

Will there be improvements without an inquiry? Perhaps, but the military have been promising reform and improvement for years. Indeed, Surrey Police have documented no fewer than seven reviews, reports and studies. Each identified similar issues relating to the vulnerability of young people at Deepcut – indeed, I understand that Brigadier Evans conducted his inquiry specifically because of the number of incidents at Deepcut. What came of that? There seems to have been relatively little follow-up.

Media pressure is mounting. On 25 April, *The Observer* ran a front page article entitled, 'Military chiefs ignored warnings over Deepcut'. It said that the Army Training and Recruiting Agency 'reported a failing in certain aspects as a result of reduction in the military workforce and increased obligations', and added that another report, underlining an absence of 'coherent and credible training activities', should be taken seriously. The *Sunday Express* also covered the story on the same day.

Some 140 Members of Parliament have signed an early-day motion supporting a full, independent inquiry into the circumstances surrounding the four deaths at Deepcut. Amnesty International backs that request. By contrast, in all the cases investigated by Surrey Police, crucial forensic and ballistics evidence was destroyed because of the Army's assumption of suicide, yet the Army continues to maintain that the investigation into Cheryl James's death was thorough.

Eight years on, Cheryl James's family still do not know how or why she died. The responsibility for that must remain with the Ministry of Defence. No matter how many reports or statistics it issues, no spin can change the fact that it failed to investigate the death of Cheryl James thoroughly, and failed in its Duty of Care. I give the Ministry of Defence credit for recognising that the families need to achieve closure, but to stop such cases from happening again the Army needs that closure too. If the MoD has nothing to hide, it is in its interest to hold an independent inquiry. It is also in the interest of every youngster who is contemplating a military career.

Statistics and internal reviews have not proved to be an acceptable alternative. For the welfare of young men and women who choose military service and for the sake of the families of the Deepcut four and those participating in the Deepcut & Beyond campaign, I respectfully ask the Secretary of State to commission an independent public inquiry into the deaths. It would be a credit to his Department if he were to do so, and nothing less can provide the answers that the families deserve and the Army needs. **[E4]**

On governmental response:

It's almost like saying 'There have been so many suspicious and unexplained circumstances of non-combat deaths in the Army, that we shouldn't really bother looking into any of them too much because it's too expensive. After all, if we accept that these deaths need to be looked into, where do you draw the line?' They say this with a straight face, more or less. Their argument being – 'That would require us to look into all the other unexplained deaths'. None of which would remain uninvestigated in civilian life.

The only explanation I can give, looking at it from the outside, for the Government's and the Military's unwillingness to go an inch further than they absolutely have to is that they must be hoping that we're going to go away and do something else. Surely, they've learned by now that isn't going to happen. Every step of the way they've given in at the last minute when they've had to and where the alternative would have been a much bigger disclosure, a much bigger public outrage. Well, the subtle but fairly obvious implication is that at every step of the way, we've uncovered something more which is bad. So, you know, what is it exactly that is so bad that they can't give it to us?

You can't reliably change the procedures if you don't reliably know what went wrong in the first place which leads to an inescapable binary conclusion and the conclusion is this: either they don't know what happened, in which case why the hell aren't they trying to find out through a full, independent public inquiry? Or they do know what happened, in which case why the hell don't they tell us?

I have been quite happy to work with Ministers in a positive way to get the answers and I've felt oftentimes that the Ministers have gone native with the Military and said, 'Well, really, we're here for the country but we're really here for you, General, and for your soldiers and for just keeping things the way that they were'. If anyone needs evidence of that, look at the endless reassurances that things have changed. Next thing we know in the press and on the television you've got video footage of people basically being tortured and then it's passed off as a 'bonding exercise'. The complete contradiction between what we're told by the authorities and what we're shown by people on the inside makes me believe that we've still got a journey here to make – but it's not nearly as big as the journey of attitude which the Government and the military need to make to sort all this out.

On the Defence Select Committee:

If this is a journey of a hundred steps, the Select Committee's report probably took us four steps forward and two steps back. It's obvious that there's a case to answer here and even the Select Committee accepted that there was some bad practice in the Army. The two steps back was how the parents ended up feeling treated by the Committee. There were some very sympathetic members of the Committee who really did understand it but there were others who obviously regarded the parents as troublemakers. Of course, yeah, these parents are troublemakers. How unreasonable for them to want to know how their kids died. How selfish of them to think that in our so-called democracy the Defence Select Committee might actually have the parents' concerns primarily on their minds. The one thing that the Select Committee did well was recognising that there was a systemic failure in the Army. But the one thing that they should have done also is to say that we can only really resolve the systemic failure in the Army if we follow a specific failure through to its conclusions and say 'these four deaths at Deepcut weren't theory. This was the practice going wrong and these specific lessons can be learned from these specific deaths and this is specifically what we need to do next.' And I think they pulled back from that. I think that was a great pity and that was a great opportunity lost.

On the Blake Review:

I remember the day when I went into the studio of Radio 4's *Today* programme and said: 'I am asking an urgent question about the state of the Army's Duty of Care, given these most recent revelations about these most recent examples of bullying in the Army'. And, lo and behold, that day, that morning, Adam Ingram announces that he's going to volunteer a statement to the House about these matters. Well, that's very nice of him but I don't for a moment imagine he'd have made that statement if we didn't have him on the ropes in that, had he not made the statement, he'd have had to answer my question and we've have had the initiative. That's how we got the Blake report.

I acted in good faith with Nicholas Blake QC. He seemed like a smart bloke, and seemed to be playing an independent hand. And all the way through, we did all we could to back him up, support his initiative publicly and to say that we would be happy enough to trust his conclusions. I have to say I was disappointed. Nicholas Blake, I think, held back from the inescapable conclusions of his own report and so while all of the evidence points in one direction – a full, independent public inquiry – Nicholas Blake chose not to call for that himself. And then it was made worse by the fact that even Nicholas Blake actually said that if there wasn't full disclosure of these reports which were being held back from the parents, then there should be an inquiry. He offered the Government a binary choice – a choice between sharing the reports or holding a full inquiry and then it all went quiet. I said in Parliament – 'Which is it going to be? The full disclosure of the reports or a full inquiry?' And the answer was C. None of the above.

On the media:

I criticised the media for taking it all at face value. I've had to sit down with members of the media, people who claim to be interested in an investigative analysis and journalists who pride themselves on being the eyes and ears of the people and they don't seem to be looking and they're not too keen on listening because it's all too complicated. Great news for the Government. If you really want to close something down, just make it really complicated so that you actually have to take a number of different points of view and read more than fifty pages. That's how it seems to me. Any journalist worth their salt could see the utter contradiction in how this has been handled. I actually think to myself – 'Well, what is it that the media's trying to do? Get to the truth or fill the pages?' You can easily fill the pages with the Government's position. There's plenty of stuff you can put in. Actually, if you want to do more than that, if you want to effect a change, then this isn't the way to do it. And I just feel sad that every time the Government's come out with something, the press have taken the Government's view and then afterwards – a couple of weeks later when we've gone round individually to each of them they go, 'Oh, yeah, I see, yeah, maybe it is a different position. But you're not going to get any further now, are you?' Why? What? Because you, the media, are too lazy to back us up on this. Oh, OK, go off and write about John Prescott playing croquet then, 'cause obviously that's much more important to the public interest than trying to figure out whether these kids were killed or not. There aren't many investigative reporters who really, really will pursue something like this. If Richard Nixon had been the Prime Minister of Britain, I get the feeling that all he would have had to do is say, 'No, no, no, no, this is how it was and I think that it would be a waste of time for anyone to investigate the Watergate further. After all, if you do that…where do you draw the line?' The media isn't against us, they're just not for anything really on this one. They just report what the Government says and they just want to move on to something simpler. Well, I think actually that's an abdication of journalistic responsibility and I think there are still a few good people and true in the media who actually will feel their conscience pricked by that. Without the media it's harder but we've got three weapons. One is the dogged determination, the absolute determination of the parents to get to the heart of this, and they haven't given up yet. Actually, I don't think they ever will give up. The second thing is the inevitability of another scandal of bullying or of failure in the Duty of Care in the Army. And thirdly as long as there are enough politicians who really care about doing the right thing, even if it's not the easy thing, then this is going to keep going on. This will keep on growing until we get to the end and it has and it will and I just don't entertain the prospect of letting go until the parents can.

I don't think power corrupts, I think power corrodes. One starts making compromises for the greater good. But at some point, unless you have a base line, unless you draw the moral line for yourself, everything's negotiable. And if everything's negotiable, then it doesn't matter who you elect, because someone can negotiate you to be exactly where they want you to be. The price might change but the destination would be the same. Now, I don't believe that in this country to look at this particular example – there is a compromise to be struck between a Duty of Care to your recruits and a fine fighting force in the field. Actually, I think we would be less likely to have accusations of bullying and mistreatment of prisoners in Iraq, if you didn't have bullying and mistreatment of soldiers in the training camps. It stands to reason. We know that domestic abuse is an inherited behaviour to an extent. Why would it be any different in the Army? I see a contradiction in expecting our Army to behave impeccably in the field but not expecting our Army to behave impeccably towards its new recruits. And, by the way, I'm not into namby-pamby health and safety obsession and everyone having a hug after a field exercise, you know, I'm not unilateralist. I'm willing to accept there are times for war – failure of politics and times for war. I'm willing to accept that there need to be secrets in Government. I have a real view of that and if I was in Government I'd expect the right to maintain secrets. I'd expect the right to vote for a war if I thought it was right. I'd expect the right to handle some matters internally. But it's back to 'where do you draw the line?' Politics is about making difficult decisions and so it's about drawing lines all the time and for me they've drawn the line in the wrong place here. They've drawn the line at 'presumed suicide' and I would draw the line at 'once we know.'

The whole thing has been a series of drives forward and knocks back. Bear in mind, the authorities have a great big fist and they can wind our campaign just about any time they want but – a bit like Muhammad Ali in the 'Rumble in the Jungle', every time he got knocked back, he got up and went back in there. And we know the outcome. So, you never know, like George Foreman – it's quite possible that the Government and the Military are going to end up selling their own brand of toasted sandwich maker and we're actually going to get the answers at the same time.

When I speak to Des James and Doreen James I see two very strong people. Two people who've grown in stature through their adversity and people who will not be cowed through the intimidating nature of coming up against the state machine. I only work for them. I work for the parents, I didn't know Cheryl James. I know that myself and the other MPs who're involved in this – we feel pretty damn strongly that if the parents are willing to carry on with this we have to do the same. And anybody else who is in my position, I would like to think as an MP, would do the same too. I think that everything that Des has been through has shown the steel of the man and shown his integrity, his eloquence and his adherence to a set of values which he's not going to be shaken off just because someone says 'Boo!' He'll do a lot of good to other people because he's been there. He has had amongst the worst experiences of any constituents I've ever had in my office and he has dealt with it with such dignity that I look at him and I think this is an exceptional man. I would love him to go into politics. I'd love him to be a Liberal Democrat but that's, you know, that's a matter for him. If he went into civic life, British politics would be gaining a great recruit. I think the guy's got a future in politics because then he actually will be in the system that's so frustrating to him. I'd love also to think that one day that would leave the door open for him to being the Secretary of State for Defence. And then maybe he can order an inquiry. **[V]**

Appendix D1

Westminster Hall adjournment debate – Tuesday 27th April 2004. Source: Hansard.

GEOFF HOON MP, Secretary of State for Defence

I begin by congratulating the Hon Member for Montgomeryshire (Lembit Öpik) on securing this debate. He has raised an important subject that has attracted considerable attention both inside and outside the House.

The events that we are discussing have one common, central truth. Four young soldiers died tragically and before their time between 1995 and 2002. The deaths of Sean Benton, Cheryl James, Geoff Gray and James Collinson represent personal tragedies for them and each of their families. They are also a source of great sadness both in the Army and throughout the services. I extend my sincere condolences to each of the families. I respect the sorrow and difficulty that they have borne over the years, I understand their desire for answers, and I accept that in some respects they have not been looked after to the highest standards that we now expect. For that, I apologise unreservedly. I share their desire to ensure that others do not suffer as they have suffered. The personal and tragic events at the heart of this debate should remain in our minds throughout.

We have heard several concerns expressed this morning, and a number of accusations have been made. However, there are two principal questions at the heart of this debate. First, do the deaths, together with deaths at other locations, somehow suggest that the Army is failing generally in its responsibilities to its young people? Secondly, do we know all that we can reasonably expect to learn about the circumstances in which the young people lost their lives?

The first question is exercising members of the Select Committee on Defence, which recently announced its inquiry into how the Armed Forces discharge their responsibilities to recruits in training. I must be careful not to pre-empt its judgments, but I hope that it will help the House if I set out the broader context of today's debate. Our Armed Forces are approximately 190,000 strong, and the Army consists of some 103,900 regular and full-time reserve personnel. Last year, 9,794 recruits passed through the Army initial training organisation and joined the field Army. Most will go on to have challenging, enjoyable and rewarding careers and will eventually leave the Army equipped with a range of skills and experiences that in many cases were beyond their hopes or expectations before they signed up.

The Army is extremely successful at training its people. It takes young people and turns them into the likes of Trooper Chris Finney, whose quick thinking and exceptional bravery last year saved the lives of his crew mates in Iraq. The ultimate and enduring proof of that is the Army's effectiveness on operations. They range from war fighting through peace support operations and counter-terrorist operations to supporting the United Kingdom civilian community in a variety of different roles. Operations take place in such diverse theatres as Iraq, Afghanistan, Sierra Leone and the Balkans. It is not an organisation unable to look after its own, reeling under the burden of systemic weaknesses in its training and support structures or incapable of self-criticism and improvement. It is a healthy institution of world renown, of which we should all be proud. The health of the Armed Forces rests on the quality of the men and women who join voluntarily. They draw their recruits from the society around them.

In training, we seek to provide not only the skills and expertise to do what is required on the battlefield but, just as important, the character to apply those skills. The Armed Forces exist to defend the nation's interests and, where necessary, to apply lethal force in that national interest. At the heart of that requirement is a need to do so in a disciplined manner.

Force is not the only means by which our Armed Forces achieve their aims. Much is spoken of the ability of our Armed Forces to win hearts and minds. That relies in no small measure on the judgment, discipline and self-confidence of the young men and women on the ground. To achieve that, their training is demanding and, necessarily, progressive. Integral to the training is the requirement to develop the ability of recruits to accept responsibility for their actions. We value our people highly and pride ourselves on the exacting standards that we maintain, both in the training that we provide and in the care that we offer.

I accept that there is risk, but the purpose of the Armed Forces is to operate and succeed in an uncertain and dangerous environment. A training regime that failed to develop individual responsibility and foster a willingness to take measured risk and address danger would fail the country. That is a point well made and recognised by my hon. Friend the Member for Blackpool, North and Fleetwood (Mrs Humble). I am grateful to her for taking the time and trouble to visit various military training establishments.

I will now deal with some of the more specific points raised by the hon. Member for Montgomeryshire. Statistical analysis has shown that, in overall terms, the number of coroner-confirmed suicides and undetermined deaths in the Armed Forces is significantly below the norm for Britain as a whole. In fact, the rate is less than half that which could be expected across the civilian population.

However, more detailed analysis has shown that more young men in the under-20 age group die in such circumstances in the Army than would be expected compared to the UK civilian population, although the small numbers involved mean that a small change can lead to a significant variation. There have been 27 such deaths over a ten-year period, against a civilian cohort of 18. That statistic is, of course, concerning and we are therefore insisting on further investigation of the subject. Ministers will continue to require that a proper explanation is given of those statistics or they must be persuaded that action has been taken to deal with whatever problem the statistics display.

Every death is deeply regrettable, and when it occurs we strive to learn lessons to ensure that, in so far as we can, processes and procedures are modified to avoid a similar incident occurring in future. The figures do not show that suicide and undetermined death are endemic in our Army. The Princess Royal Barracks at Deepcut has come under particular scrutiny. There have been four tragic deaths there in the past nine years. That is, certainly, four too many. The death of Private Sean Benton in 1995 was the first at that establishment since 1965.

There is no doubt that bullying is insidious and corrosive and is the very antithesis of the principle of self-discipline and the concept of teamwork on which so much of the success of the Armed Forces is founded. I accept that there is a fine line between unnecessarily overbearing behaviour and the robust approach to training and discipline that the Armed Forces have to take to prepare their people for the harsh environment in which they may be asked to operate. That is a line that the Armed Forces are well practised at treading. No one should be in any doubt that bullying has no place in the Army or the Armed Forces. It is rooted out whenever and wherever it is discovered.

There have been many assertions in the media and elsewhere of systemic bullying in the Army. Our policy of zero tolerance to bullying is simply that. It does not mean that bullying does not occur. We can, and do, make our policy clear, but even with the best regime in the world, bullying may occur. Where we are aware of it, we will deal with it robustly. What we cannot do is investigate rumour and hearsay. Without the co-operation of those affected, we cannot succeed. Those who allege bullying must come forward. I assure hon. Members that allegations properly made will be thoroughly investigated.

Of course it is right to probe, to verify and to seek improvements. That is what this debate is about. During the course of their investigations, Surrey Police provided some helpful suggestions about how to discharge the Army's care responsibilities. Their work in the supporting investigation by the Deputy Adjutant General has produced real changes in the way we work.

I want to pick out a few of the measures that have already been taken. We have accepted that the ratio of recruits to instructors rose far too high in the mid-1990s, particularly in phase 2 establishments. Ratios in excess of 50:1 were not untypical then, but that has now been directly addressed with the provision of an additional 179 instructors in the training organisation. The target ratio of 38:1 is being achieved or exceeded in all phase 1 and phase 2 training establishments. That change is already having a real effect.

The situation of soldiers awaiting trade training – SATT – in which recruits are required to wait between completing one trade course and starting the next, has been cited as one of the potential causes of frustration, anxiety and lack of focus among young recruits. I can report some significant improvements on that. SATT figures are now at an all-time low right across the Army's training organisation.

Guarding routines were identified by the deputy adjutant general as a substantial contributory factor in the level of opportunity risk to young recruits, specifically at Deepcut. Day-to-day responsibility for managing the guarding function at the Deepcut site now falls to the Military Provost Guard Service, which is also taking on an increasing proportion of guarding duties.

That has significantly reduced the burden on trainees and the opportunity risk identified in the DAG's report.

In addition, the MoD director of operational capability has examined the initial training of non-officer recruits across all three services. That work has produced 58 different recommendations, the majority of which have been implemented. Others still require funding, but we are addressing that and making progress. The director's report has established a co-ordinated system for the identification and application of best practice in initial training across all three services.

I hope that hon. Members will accept that that amounts to a persuasive case that the MoD is not failing, that its leaders are not complacent but are taking their responsibilities seriously and that we remain sensitive to the needs of our people. I am happy for that to be tested by others and therefore welcome the Defence Committee's interest in the same way that I welcomed the analysis in the fifth report of the Chief Constable of the Surrey Police, which was published last month. He acknowledged our efforts to secure improvements, but he was far from uncritical. He believed that we could have been quicker at learning lessons from the two earlier deaths. He went further by saying that, although it is clear that a change process has been initiated, in his view 'a broader enquiry is necessary to provide assurance that the current momentum in the development and implementation of regime improvements is sustained'. He went on to suggest, among other things, that the inquiry should consider 'how independent oversight might help the Army define and maintain appropriate standards of care for young soldiers'.

The issues raised are complex and have significant implications. We are not yet in a position to announce what action we intend to take in response. I am sorry if that proves frustrating for the families and for hon. Members, but this is not a case of prevarication. Several factors must be considered and we are determined to get this right. For example, the possibility of engaging with an external organisation to provide some independent oversight of our training arrangements and the discharge of our care responsibilities has certain attractions, but we must think carefully about which organisation would be best qualified to carry out such a role and what should be the limits of its responsibilities. It will be a challenging task, which will require experience of care issues, ideally in relation to young adults, and Armed Forces training, as well as a demonstrable independence from the MoD.

In addition, my right hon. Friend the Minister of State is anxious to meet all four families before final decisions are made. He has already met two of the families and is in contact with a third family about a meeting in the near future. I hope that we will be in position to make an announcement to the House next month on the way ahead.

Each of the four families has suffered a grievous loss that will affect them for the rest of their lives.

It is clear that in certain respects the support that we provided to grieving relatives fell short of the standards that we demand of ourselves. I extend my sincerest apologies to the families for the additional pain that that caused. It is clear that each family feels poorly served not only by the institution whose responsibility it was to protect their loved ones but by those who were responsible for finding out what happened. That said, the deaths and the actions taken in response to them have been subject to thorough and detailed examination. Surrey Police spent 15 months and have been assiduous in their scrutiny of each case. They declared that they had no intention of pursuing any criminal charges in respect of the deaths. Their press release of 19 September 2003 stated: 'Despite the scale of the investigation, no evidence has come to light so far to indicate any prospect of a prosecution directly related to these deaths'. Their conclusion on causation was clear.

A coroner's inquest provides the established route by which the legal right to a public investigation following a death is satisfied. Inquests into three of the deaths have already been held, and the coroner has confirmed that the Surrey Police investigation brought to light no new evidence that would warrant him seeking to open new inquests in these cases. He will in due course examine the circumstances of the fourth death – that of James Collinson. Internally the Army has commissioned two Boards of Inquiry and made the findings known to the families. It will convene a third and fourth when the coroner has completed his work.

I therefore see several difficulties associated with the kind of inquiry proposed in the debate, and I return to the second of my initial questions. What could a narrowly focused inquiry reveal about the circumstances of individual deaths that successive internal and external inquiries have not? What evidence is a further inquiry likely to uncover that has not already come to light, particularly with the passage of time since the first two incidents? What reasonable grounds are there for suspecting that the truth, in so far as it is knowable, has not already been established?

I wonder, too, whether there is a uniformity of view among those calling for a public inquiry about what such an inquiry would cover. If an inquiry were to focus on the individual circumstances surrounding specific incidents, should it relate to the four deaths in question, or, as has been suggested, have a wider remit to investigate other deaths in other locations? If the latter, which and why, and where should a line be drawn?

The intended purpose of such an inquiry is to get closer to the truth about what happened; I ask how realistic that is. If the purpose is to reveal weaknesses in procedure and inadequacies in the Army's handling of the families, which appear to be the basis of the case presented by the hon. Member for Montgomeryshire, it is arguable that its work has already been done and its conclusions already accepted. Errors were made, which I hope will never be repeated. I accept that we are still not yet as good as we should be as far as this matter is concerned, but we have worked hard to put things right and we continue to work hard to implement the wider lessons.

In conclusion, I assure the House once again that my ministerial colleagues, the Army chain of command and I are acutely aware of the sensitivity of these issues and the continued public and parliamentary interest in them. We deeply regret the death of anyone in our charge; we recognise that we have a duty to the families of those who have died and we apologise unreservedly where that duty has not been fully discharged. We know that there is nothing that we can do to restore loved ones to their families; what we can do is continue to ensure not only that our house is in order, but that it is demonstrably so.

This is a theme that my right hon. Friend the Minister of State with responsibility for the Armed Forces will take up in more detail when he makes an announcement to the House in the coming weeks. In the meantime, we continue to demonstrate that we have nothing to hide. We co-operated fully with the Surrey Police and gave them full access to our archives; the joint Army-Police learning account, which is a mechanism for recording lessons learned and tracking progress made in implementing them, is testament to that co-operation.

Now that the Police investigation is concluded, we intend to give similar access to the wider public. Many of the documents on which the chief constable drew in his fifth report are now in the public domain. We published those documents; they were not dragged out of us.

We have for some months been encouraging hon. Members to visit training establishments, and seven have so far been visited, but the take-up for the programme has been low. We continue to stress the importance of hon. Members seeing for themselves what life is like for recruits in training, and how we approach the training task.

One further visit is currently planned, which will take place on 16 June and will include Princess Royal barracks, Deepcut and the Army training regiment at Winchester. Other visits will be arranged subject to take-up so that as many as possible can take advantage of these opportunities and see for themselves what an outstanding job the Army does in training its people. **[E4]**

Appendix D2

House of Commons debate – Wednesday 29th March 2006. Source: Hansard.

ADAM INGRAM MP, Minister of State (Armed Forces):

On 15 December 2004, I informed the House that I had commissioned a review into the circumstances surrounding the deaths of four young soldiers at Princess Royal barracks, Deepcut, during the period 1995 to 2002. As I told the House then, I was aware that its scope and nature may not satisfy all those, including hon. Members, who have been calling for a formal public inquiry into combat deaths in the Armed Forces, especially the four deaths at Deepcut. I said that by concentrating on the circumstances of the four deaths, the review would focus on the issue at the heart of current public concern.

The review has been undertaken by the distinguished human rights lawyer, Mr Nicholas Blake QC, and is now complete. Copies will be placed in the Libraries of both Houses. This morning, the families had the benefit of a briefing by Mr Blake on his conclusions. I know that this will be another difficult day for them; the passage of time, in such sad circumstances, does little to lessen the pain. I hope that they will find at least that Mr Blake has addressed carefully and sensitively the questions that have troubled them. I acknowledge the dignity with which they have conducted themselves over this long period.

I am grateful to Mr Blake for the thorough and professional way in which he has approached his task. In conducting his review, he has had the full co-operation of the Ministry of Defence. He has had full and unrestricted access to our records, and all serving and retired soldiers were encouraged to help the review in any way they could. I am satisfied that the report, which runs to 416 pages, plus annexes, represents an independent, objective and comprehensive analysis of all matters that have a bearing on the four deaths, and that Mr Blake has not been constrained by his terms of reference. Importantly, he has been able to tackle the wider issues.

There were three issues about which much comment had been made on events at Deepcut: the alleged suspicious circumstances of the deaths, a claimed culture of bullying and the need for a formal public inquiry. I am pleased to note that Mr Blake makes substantial findings on all three points. First, he has concluded that, on the balance of probabilities, the deaths of Sean Benton, Cheryl James and Geoff Gray at Deepcut were self-inflicted. Given the recent coroner's inquest into the death of James Collinson, he understandably refrains from reaching any conclusion on that particular death. However, he comments that the opportunity for self-infliction was afforded by the policy of frequently assigning trainees at Deepcut to guard duty, unsupervised by experienced soldiers.

The review found a number of factors that may have contributed to the trainees' unhappiness and may have made them more susceptible to self-harm. The review considers that 'although the Army did not cause any of the deaths', there were institutional failures to identify potential sources of risk and subsequently to address them. On the question of bullying, Mr Blake states that there is no evidence that any of the trainees were bullied to death.

However, he accepts that some trainees at Deepcut – probably only a small minority – experienced harassment, discrimination and oppressive behaviour. Those who did not complain appear to have had little confidence that the system could or would address their grievances. These are important criticisms, which will be addressed.

Finally, on the question of a public inquiry, as I indicated in my response to the earlier House of Commons Defence Committee on this matter, I did not consider that a formal public inquiry was required. The Defence Committee was of a similar view. In a carefully reasoned examination of the arguments for such an approach, Mr Blake has concluded that a public inquiry into the immediate or broader circumstances surrounding these deaths is not necessary. I reaffirm my earlier position and concur with his conclusion.

This review, taken alongside the other inquiries and inquests into the deaths at Deepcut, has set out with great clarity the circumstances of the four deaths and the context in which they occurred. We now need to move on and take forward the changes that are required. We accept Mr Blake's conclusions and welcome the opportunity to address his recommendations. We accept that there have been shortcomings, and we will do all that we can to address them.

Although the purpose of the review was not to attribute blame, Mr Blake has described a disturbing catalogue of allegations of misconduct at the relevant times. The Army authorities will carefully examine the report to see whether there is any indication of professional misconduct or negligence that might make administrative action appropriate. In addition, any matters that suggest that a disciplinary offence may have been committed will be referred to the Royal Military Police for further investigation. We will also have to take into account the overall training environment in which our personnel were working and the constraints faced by those in the command chain.

Mr Blake understands the importance, particularly for the Army, of recruiting under-18s, but he has highlighted weaknesses with regard to their appropriate care. We are alive to that issue and we are improving the standard of care and support afforded to young recruits. For example, trainees' surveys have been established and a note of guidance for all commanding officers covering all aspects of working with under-18s has been produced. Furthermore, Mr Blake particularly commends the specialist training regimes for 16-year-olds established at the Army Training Regiment, Bassingbourn, and the Army foundation college, Harrogate. However, there is clearly still more to do, especially in extending best practices such as those at these establishments, and we are committed to implementing such changes as far and as quickly as we can.

The quality of our Armed Forces and the professional way in which they were, and are, meeting their operational commitments is evidence of the quality of military training, and I pay tribute to that without hesitation. The report describes the British Army as a unique and extraordinary institution. For the past decade or more, it has been sent on a wide variety of operational deployments in many parts of the world, involving great personal danger and regular personal sacrifice.

The report notes that many of the young people who are, or were, accepted as recruits into the Army have had very challenging lives as children. A high proportion were from single-parent homes, some had left school with no qualifications, and many had deficits in basic skills. The report comments that it is a remarkable challenge to turn these young people into effective soldiers forming part of a disciplined and interdependent team. It is worth noting that Deepcut alone sent approximately 10,000 trainees into the field Army during the period covered by the review.

However, the number of young people, particularly those under 18, that the services employ places particular responsibilities on us to recognise their potential vulnerability. We are committed to improving the way in which all our recruits are trained, developed and looked after. In view of that, and in light of the recommendations made in previous recent reports by the Defence Committee and the adult learning inspectorate, work has already been done, and continues to be done, to make changes for the better.

As in society as a whole, bullying, harassment and other inappropriate behaviour can never be totally eliminated in the Armed Forces. However, it is essential that we establish an environment in which bullying is wholly unacceptable. At every stage of their training and careers, it is made very clear to personnel that bullying and harassment, in any form, is not tolerated, and that it is part of their duty, and a function of leadership, to eliminate it.

It is a sad and unfortunate fact – again, just as in wider society – that the Armed Forces will never be able to eradicate the tragic incidence of suicide or self-harm. However, the risks can be reduced to a minimum by careful management, pragmatic policies and better understanding, knowledge and education. As the Blake review makes clear: 'Every Officer, NCO, civilian instructor and trainee should be alert to any sign of abuse and be required to report it through the chain of Command, so prompt and effective action can be taken'.

The Armed Forces Bill, currently being scrutinised by a Select Committee of this House, contains proposals to streamline the complaints redress system, including provision for an independent element. Also, the Bill will consider aspects of the procedures applying to Boards of Inquiry. The review makes recommendations in those two important areas. We will give full consideration to those recommendations, and the Bill gives us the opportunity to implement any changes deemed appropriate.

The report has identified areas in the training environment, especially between 1995 and 2002, that required improvement. It cites examples of inappropriate behaviour that should not have taken place. It also identifies areas where we can, and should, improve the way in which we manage the young people for whom we are responsible, and we accept those observations. We now need to look at every one of Mr Blake's 34 detailed recommendations to see how they should best be taken forward to address the weaknesses identified as quickly and as effectively as possible. I also urge right hon. and hon. Members to take time to analyse Mr Blake's report in full prior to forming their own opinions.

Mr Blake has given us a detailed and painstaking report of considerable substance. I am confident that it will provide further impetus for improvement. I can assure the House of my determination to deal with the issues that he has raised, and I undertake to provide a detailed formal written response to the House on all the recommendations. I am determined to ensure that everything possible is done to prevent similar tragedies occurring in the future.

I have enormous confidence in the dedicated men and women working as instructors in our training organisation. I want to make sure that they have the support, the resources and the facilities that they need to pursue excellence. The trained young men and women they produce lie at the very core of how we deliver on the defence interests of this country. Their efforts have to be matched by commitment from the very top of the MoD.

Mr Blake concluded his report with his profound condolences to each of the families concerned. On behalf of the Ministry of Defence, I again add my condolences. **[E4]**

Afterword
by Des James

It was so difficult to write this.

The desire to tell the entire story in minute detail is immense, to explain what a beautiful child Cheryl was, her smile, her giggles, her caring, her compassion, her sense of humour, her energy...but when I try to do that, it is all soured by the appalling, disgusting way in which her death was dismissed by the authorities in 1995: how communication with the MoD, the Army, even the Coroner was simply closed down early in 1996; and how it all started over again in 2002. The hopes we had then that finally there would be an explanation, or at least a process that would pursue that explanation until pursuance was wasted, and every piece of even an incomplete jigsaw was in place.

Dominique de Menil, an American art collector and museum founder is credited with saying: *'What should move us to action is human dignity, the inalienable dignity of the oppressed, but also the dignity of each of us. We lose dignity if we tolerate the intolerable.'* I found those words so appropriate when applied to the scandal that is Deepcut. What Harry and Linda Benton, Geoff and Diane Gray, Jim and Yvonne Collinson, Doreen and I have had to experience *should* be intolerable in a civilised society.

I sometimes wonder what would have happened if the press had not picked up on the story in 2002, if the realisation there had been four deaths at Deepcut had been further delayed. It may have taken another four years, or five years? One thing is very clear though, if God forbid there had been more deaths, this Government would not have had a public inquiry. It was clear from the start, as soon as the media forced the agenda; the Government began their counter agenda to prevent an inquiry no matter what. I still do not know why and I probably never will; it makes you wonder what was it that drove them to act as they did.

Surrey Police were forced into a knee-jerk re-investigation which they had neither planned nor budgeted and which they expected, at worse, to take a few months to complete. It gave the Government some breathing space ('we could not possibly comment while the Surrey Police investigation is ongoing').

When the Surrey Police investigation was (deservedly) discredited, the Government had to find another comfort blanket to hide behind while the public outrage died down. Adam Ingram, the Minster of State for the Armed Forces, found quite a few comfort blankets over the following months and years: the DAG Report, the DOC Report, the Devon & Cornwall police review, the House of Commons Defence Select Committee Inquiry (not into Deepcut of course) and the ridiculous ALI inspections.

Despite all of these carefully choreographed initiatives, media pressure for a public inquiry continued until Ingram announced his final initiative in

December 2004. The Nicholas Blake Review was to be the Government's ultimate comfort blanket.

In short, Blake interviewed four politicians, three non-commissioned officers who were at Deepcut, eight officers who were at Deepcut and no less than 21 very senior officers, none of whom had been at Deepcut. He did not speak to any recruit who had been at the camp at the time of the deaths. There was no cross-examination, no possibility to challenge evidence, no opportunity even to challenge the Review process itself.

Today Adam Ingram's successor, Bob Ainsworth, refuses even to speak to the families about the Blake report. So there we have it.

A camp that was so out of control; that created a culture where bullying and inappropriate sexual activity were common place; where self-harm, some recorded, most missed, went on unabated; and where ultimately four innocent young people with their lives ahead of them were unceremoniously shot dead. A Government that worked so hard to prevent a proper inquiry, that danced around justice until the media finally switched the lights off.

A simple question remains for the families, for recruits in the future, for the society we belong to, that if we do not take the trouble to find out how the corrupt culture of Deepcut 1995-2002 evolved, *how can we possibly know that the preventative measures the MoD alleges are now in place, are in fact enough to prevent this all happening again?*

The Blake Review was published on March 29, 2006.

> *'It was made plain that my terms of reference included the ability to make recommendations to you addressing issues arising in my Review of the circumstances surrounding the deaths. I have made 34 recommendations.'*
>
> *Nicholas Blake, March 29, 2006*

Blake's 34th recommendation was *not* to have a public inquiry.

No matter what comes in the future, we will always be grateful for the genuine interest in our story and the dogged determination with which Philip Ralph pursued this project. A number of writers came and went, some spending hours, even days with us before, for various reasons, ending their interest. Philip has delivered and it has been such a support to us to experience, and of course share, his passionate interest in the Deepcut story. We will always consider him a friend. Cheryl would have approved as well!

Des James, June 2008

Eulogy for Cheryl James
written by her father

The following epitaph was written by Cheryl's father in the dreadful days following her death, the description of Cheryl will be very familiar to family and friends, but may also help those who did not know her to understand our loss.

You all have your own personal memories of Cheryl our little girl.

She came to us from the head of two queues, the one handing out compassion and caring, and the one handing out cheeky smiles. Those two qualities became her trademark – if you wanted one you had the other for free. Cheryl enjoyed a wonderfully happy childhood, collecting animals as waifs and strays as though it were her sole responsibility for the world, and while so many of us plummeted to the depths of despair last Monday, Shep, Buff and others too countless to mention will have regained their best friend ever.

As a teenager Cheryl confronted a few more hurdles than any of us could have expected to be placed before her, but surrounded by a love that only Mums and Dads and families understand she cleared them all with yards to spare. An indomitable spirit and that wonderful, wonderful smile, she had no idea *how* to be second. By the age of seventeen she had worked part-time in three old people's homes, and showed a caring for them quite unique in someone so young. She worried so much about people – not only what they thought of her, an expected characteristic that comes with the vanity of youth – but about them. How they were? What she could do and would they be all right? So, from the child who saved pigeons, sparrows and so many others she drove us to distraction, Cheryl had matured in to a young lady whose caring began to map out her life for her. And the cheeky smile followed.

Cheryl loved the Army. She would return home on leave like a juggernaut of enthusiasm, turn the house inside out and upside down within 48 hours and then worry about which friends she may have hurt because she had not got in touch with them while she was home. Her Passing Out parade was a landmark in all our lives, she knew and we knew the final hurdle was cleared. By a mile. The worries and tribulations of teenage years were over and she had achieved that little bit extra. No second place. That day the smile were it possible, was more wonderful than ever. Cheryl completed her basic training and obtained an HGV license before her eighteenth birthday – she was so pleased – not that she had achieved but that she had achieved at an age and a stage in her career when it might not have been expected. No second place.

On one of her last visits home we discussed when at the age of fourteen a colleague of mine from work had visited us. He and Cheryl got on famously and at one point in the evening the challenges were flying! These culminated in a game of chess, and Cheryl was not as dominant in the game as she would have wished. Not so dominant anyway as to prevent John's playful taunts. John is now a company Factory Manager in Taiwan and I reminded Cheryl he would be coming home for Christmas. 'Is he?' she said – 'Great… ask him can he drive a lorry!' That cheeky smile was as bright as the sun! [02]